Because He Said So

Discovering Who the I AM Says I Am

FORTY-DAY DEVOTIONAL

Missy Washam

ISBN: 978-1-7360682-0-5 (Paperback edition)
Copyright Number: 1-9910971351

Printed by Kindle Direct Publishing in the United States of America

Design by Hannah Thomas

 Fireflies Publishing Co.

www.IAmBecauseHeSaidSo.com

To the strongest woman I know,
my mom, Lottie Vance. Thanks for
introducing me to Jesus.
I love you!

Table of Contents

Hello Sister!

Thank you for joining me on this journey to *believe* that you are, indeed, who He says you are. The fact that you have this book in your hand, means I already consider you a friend. I call you "sister" because we have the same Heavenly Father. Also, for my entire life, I have thought of my girlfriends as my sisters. By the end of our forty days together my desire is that you will consider me a friend and a sister as well.

The first thing I want you to know is that this book is for **you**. Within the pages, you will find a safe place to grow in Christ. No matter where you are on your journey with Jesus, I believe the message of this book will deepen your connection with Him. Whether you are just beginning to explore what it means to be a believer, you are wanting to grow in your relationship with Christ, or you can't recall a day in your life without Him, my fervent prayer is that these words will richly bless you. My hope is that this book will help you see how loved and adored you are by your Heavenly Father. I want this to be a springboard for your heart to be awakened to a firm belief that *His* word, *His* view of you, and what *He* has in store for you is true. And I pray that you realize THAT is all that truly matters.

Love and abundant blessings,

Missy ♡

Preface

Some of my earliest memories include Jesus and are set in sunny, warm Orlando, Florida where we lived the first few years of my life. I remember so vividly, riding to church on Sunday mornings in my mom's yellow Chevy Vega with the windows rolled down. She drove us to service each week and would sing along with me as I belted out some of my favorite children's church songs: *Jesus Loves Me, This Little Light of Mine, Deep and Wide,* and *Jesus Loves the Little Children of the World.*

Around the age of 13, I officially accepted His gift of salvation. Although I wish that I could share with you that BIG moment, that "Kumbaya" type moment, that so many have when they find Jesus, I can't. That was not my experience. The best illustration of my life with Jesus is more like a cup placed under a dripping faucet that slowly fills to the rim with water and then overflows. I have always had a Bible nearby. I have always thanked Him for the food that I ate and the blessings that He has given me. I have always prayed to Him during times of need and moments of desperation, and I have always sung to Him in praise. I'm so grateful to have known Jesus my entire life.

My significant "A-HA" moment didn't come until my mid-forties when I stepped out of my comfort zone and made two decisions that would forever change my life. I became a certified speaker, coach, and trainer with The John Maxwell Team, and then my childhood best friend, Dayna Curtis Moseley, and I gathered about twenty of our friends together for a forty-day prayer journey. I had no idea what God would do through these two new endeavors, but it didn't take long for Him to reveal Himself. He began opening opportunities for me to connect with women who were looking to know Him on a deeper level, an authentic level. And, that small group of twenty women that Dayna and I started, grew to thousands of women and became what is now known as Soul Sisters Ministry. Soul Sisters serves women, globally, through daily devotionals/blogs, prayer posts, retreats, service projects, and local group meetings. (You can connect with Soul Sisters at https://www.facebook.com/groups/soulsistersministry or at soulsistersministry.com)

It wasn't until I was speaking to and with women from all over the world that I had *my* moment of understanding. I was pouring the truth of Christ's love and sacrifice into these women in hopes that they would understand how much they were loved and adored by their Heavenly Father. I was praying that, through the truth in His Word, they would recognize that they were created ON purpose and FOR a purpose.

Then it hit me like a ton of bricks. I realized that I passionately believed all of what I was sharing was true for THEM, but I was not confident that it applied to ME. I was sharing that YOU are loved, YOU are forgiven, YOU are called, and YOU are equipped. All the while I was questioning if I was worthy of His love! I tried to fill in the blank for my own life, "I am _____. " But I couldn't do it because I was so accustomed to thinking of myself and speaking to myself in negative ways. It didn't feel like His truth applied to me personally.

I knew from my experiences and many conversations that other women were fighting the same battle of believing that God's truths were for them. I now recognized that I needed to believe His truths as well. After all, how could I pour into others if I wasn't confident that what I was sharing with them was true for everyone, *including* myself. I felt God calling me to write a book about believing that God's truths and promises are for all of us. But how? How could I believe it? How could I *write* about it? I was fighting the enemy, the world, and even my own negative thoughts. Sister, the struggle was real.

Everything changed when God woke me up one cold November night and told me *why* I should believe that His promises were as true for me as they were for others. He spoke four words into my heart, "Because I said so!" Isn't our Lord wonderful? With these few words, He answered the question in my mind using words that He *knew* I would understand! You see, I grew up in the south. In my neck of the woods, it's a known fact that when you asked your mom or dad "Why?" they would reply with the same answer. Every. Single. Time. "Because I said so", and that was it! No more questions to be asked, you simply did what you were told because of their authority. And, because God is the *ultimate* authority, THE I AM, I can believe everything that He says about me. Why? Because **He** said so! **THE I AM** says I am! And thus, the title of this book was born.

I began praying and searching for the evidence of who I am in Him through scripture. I journaled each verse and I knew that His words could be trusted. But it still wasn't easy to believe His words were for *me* because simply *knowing* the truth is not enough. I had to meditate on His word. I had to bombard my thoughts with His promises and guard my tongue from negative self-talk. Through this process I began to believe that I am who He says I am. I will tell you, however, that it is a process that takes practice. I know that the voices of the world will invade my heart and mind if I don't seek Him first every day and remind myself daily who I am in Him.

During our journey, I will share with you the proof, through scripture, of who you are in Him. But, as I stated earlier, knowing won't be enough. You must change your thoughts and the words you speak. (Proverbs 23:7 and 18:21) You must begin to think of yourself like God thinks of you and speak to yourself as God speaks of you! This book will guide you in this process by leading you to focus daily on His Word and claim forty God-firmations, affirmations of who you are in Christ. Through the practice of becoming more like Him and trusting that you are who He says you are, the strongholds and self-limiting beliefs that the enemy uses to separate you from Him will begin to fade. Everything in your life will begin to change. Make no mistake about it… **this book is not about thinking more of yourself - it's about thinking more of God**. It's about believing Him, growing in relationship with Him, and taking the right steps in all the things He calls you to do in His name – big things and small things.

So, Sister, are you ready? I'm praying for you over these next forty days. I'm praying that you change your thoughts and your words to be more like His. My prayer is that in believing Him completely, you will experience the abundant life that He came to give you. (John 10:10) Let's go! Let's begin the journey with God that has the power to transform your life and can become the catalyst to cause a ripple effect of change in the lives of everyone you meet. Let's do it…because He said so!

Day 1

I am a...
MASTERPIECE

> *"For we are God's masterpiece. He has created us anew in Christ Jesus, so we can do the good things he planned for us long ago."*
>
> **Ephesians 2:10**

For most people, the word "masterpiece" conjures up thoughts about famous works of art and the artists who created them: da Vinci and the Mona Lisa, Michelangelo and the Sistine Chapel, van Gogh and Starry Night, just to name a few. These masterpieces are handmade, one of a kind, and worth millions of dollars.

As a 4-year-old at Kindercastle Preschool, I remember suiting up in my smock and stepping into the role of artist when I was creating my first masterpiece, a Christmas gift for my mom. My teacher, Mrs. Shelly, was giving us instructions as she passed out our supplies. She told us to think through what we wanted to paint, and do it carefully, because there were only enough supplies for each of us to get one canvas. I knew what I wanted to paint — a picture of my mom. I carefully chose each color and painted every line with precision. When I finished, I was proud of my work. I could hardly wait to give this piece of art to my mother and see her eyes light up. And light up they did! She made me feel like my work was the most beautiful piece of art she had ever seen. Looking at it now, from an adult perspective, I realize that it was nothing more than scribbles (see Appendix 1). It was far from a masterpiece. It was a mess! However, despite the fact that the picture was imperfect, my mom treasured it as a masterpiece just the same.

Because of Jesus and the sacrifice that He made for us, God sees the imperfect as perfect *and our messiness as a* masterpiece.

Your Heavenly Father intentionally created you just as you are, in His image, to be His masterpiece. He doesn't make mistakes; He doesn't make junk. So why is it that so often, when you look in the mirror, you rarely, if ever, see a masterpiece? If you are like me, the image you see is marred by the messy lines of your mistakes and the scribbles of your shortcomings. Everyone has them. They are the marks that sin and shame leave on your life. And, oh, how the evil one wants you to believe that your past depreciates your present value. But, because of Jesus and the sacrifice that He made for you, God sees the imperfect as perfect and your messiness as a masterpiece. God can use you to complete His good work, the work He created in you before you were even born! "For you created my inmost being; you knit me together in my mother's womb" (Psalm 139:13). Jesus' blood has cleansed the canvas of your life and erased your sins. Those sins can no longer taint the masterpiece that you are.

During the next 40 days you are going to discover how God is continually forming you into the masterpiece He created you to be. There's no doubt about it; the Creator of the Universe is an artist like none other. Everything He creates is a unique work of art, a masterpiece. I encourage you to cling to and trust in God's word while striving to "think like He thinks" and "speak like He speaks."

So today and every day moving forward, when you look in the mirror and you feel like the scribbled art of a 4-year old or a Picasso with all of your pieces out of place, stand tall, smile back at the reflection in the mirror, and declare, **"I am a masterpiece... because He said so!"**

Prayer

Dear Lord, Please forgive me for getting discouraged when I look in the mirror and can't see beyond my faults and my failures. Remind me, Father, that You created me in Your own image so that I could be like You. Thank You for seeing my potential instead of my mistakes. Help me see myself through Your eyes, as Your masterpiece. In Jesus' name and for the Father's glory, Amen.

READ MORE

God's Word says you are a masterpiece...

Genesis 1:26 • Genesis 1:31 • Psalm 139:14

Ephesians 1:4 • 2 Timothy 2:21

If God was able create an amazing world out of something that was "formless and empty", can anything keep Him from turning your life into a masterpiece? **List areas of your life that you feel are messy and turn them over to God believing that He can transform them.**

Daily Challenge:

#masterpiece

☐ Download the song "Who You Say I Am" by Hillsong Worship and let the lyrics fill your soul. Listen to it often over the next 40 Days and ongoing to remind you who He says you are.

☐ Share a video, image, or your written testimony with other sisters in Christ in the "Because He Said So" Facebook group. Please use the hashtags #masterpiece and #iambecausehesaidso on all social media posts.

Visit Facebook.com/groups/iambecausehesaidso to join the community!

Day 2

I am...

KNOWN

"O LORD, you have examined my heart and know everything about me."

Psalm 139:1

I love to go to concerts. There is something that is thrilling about being shoulder-to-shoulder with other fans listening to someone perform songs live. There is an energy that can't be replicated by recorded music. Most of the concerts I have attended were performed by extremely famous people. I've been lucky to have seen some all-time great performers. I was thrilled to see Paul McCartney, Lionel Richey, Carrie Underwood, Elton John, Faith Hill, Garth Brooks and Lauren Daigle just to name a few. I've been at a few concerts where the superstar has acknowledged individuals in the audience and called them by name to join them on the stage. WOW! To be known by a legend—that would be amazing!

The truth is, everyone wants to be known. The way you are known by others ranges from the less personal of being recognized simply by your face to a bit more personal of being able to recall your name. There are those acquaintances that you have in your life who know a few of the details about you, and then there are those with whom you share a deep meaningful relationship. These people know who you are to the depths of your soul.

I'd say the majority of the people who know us tend to be on the less personal side of the spectrum. Think Facebook. Think Instagram. Oh, you call them "friends" and you may have hundreds or even thousands of them. But they only know you by the information you share or "post". They don't really know you. You must build relationships to be truly known. Relationships are built on shared experiences over time. I pray you have people in your life that really know you; the ones with whom you avoid making eye contact in certain situations because you would both burst out laughing at the worst possible moment if you looked at each other. The ones who can finish your sentences and know what you're thinking without saying a word. The ones who know you love being swept away to Sonic for their famous cherry limeade when you're having a bad day. It seems as if these types of intimate relationships are few and far between. In fact, for some it may be easier to not pursue these deeper types of connections and just have "acquaintances", because if you really let someone know you, you take the chance that they may not always like what they see.

> Sister, I am here to tell you that God, the Creator of the Universe, The Alpha and The Omega knows *your* name.

Earlier I mentioned how cool it would be to have a superstar know you and call you by name. But, the truth is—they are only people just like you and me. Sister, I am here to tell you that God, The Creator of the Universe, The Alpha and The Omega knows your name. How much better is it to be known by Him than an earthly legend? Your Father knows you intimately. He knows your face; He knows all the details of your life. He knows the public stuff and He knows the private stuff that you keep deep inside and don't share with anyone. Scripture teaches that "He not only knows your name, but He knows the intimate details of your life down to the number of hairs that are on your head" (Luke 12:7). As you see from today's spotlight scripture, He knows your heart and everything about you. WOW! How wonderful it is to know that the King of kings and Lord of lords, knows you by name, loves you despite of your shortcomings, and actually sacrificed His own son's life for yours.

So today and every day moving forward, when you feel like you are unseen, unimportant or unknown, take the time to remind yourself that He knows your name, and then repeat out loud, "**I am known...because He said so!**"

Prayer

Dear Lord, Forgive me when I focus more on being popular with people than on the fact that You, the Creator of the Universe, know me. It amazes me that, despite Your awareness of all my inadequacies, You love me. I want to know You more, Father, so that I can help others who don't yet know You, discover Your love. In Jesus' name and for the Father's glory, Amen.

READ MORE

God's Word says you are known...

Isaiah 43:1-3 • Jeremiah 1:5 • Luke 12:6-8

1 Corinthians 8:3 • 2 Timothy 2:19

Are you beginning to understand that the most famous person in history knows you and wants a closer relationship with you? **What can you do each day to let God know that you want to be closer to Him and know Him more?**

Daily Challenge:

#known

☐ Write your autograph on a piece of paper. Put today's verse underneath it and stick the paper in your Bible. Use this for years to remember that God knows you by name.

☐ Share a video, image, or your written testimony with other sisters in Christ in the "Because He Said So" Facebook group. Use the hashtag #known and #iambecausehesaidso

Visit Facebook.com/groups/iambecausehesaidso to join the community!

Day 3

I am... LOVED

"For God so loved the world that he gave his one and only Son, that whoever believes in him shall not perish but have eternal life."

John 3:16

I remember when my husband, Chris, first told me that he loved me. It was December 14, 1988. We were at a party surrounded by people, and he wrote it in my hand: "I ♥ U"! My soul was soaring!

Oh, to be loved! It's what every human being craves above anything else. It doesn't matter how beautiful, successful, or wealthy you are - without love, life is meaningless. "I Will Always Love You", "Endless Love", "How Deep Is Your Love?", "Love Will Keep Us Together", and "Will You Still Love Me Tomorrow?" are just a few of the songs from the list of the Top 100 Love Songs of All Time. The total number of songs written on the subject of love is in excess of 97 million. And just think of all the poems and novels written on the topic. Love is definitely a popular subject.

There's no doubt about it, the three words everyone longs to hear are "I love you!" And, oh, how the devil uses your quest for love to defeat you every day. It seems as though society is continually reminding you that you aren't good enough to be loved just the way you are. Everyone in the modern world is told that you must try to be more, do more, and have more so that you can land love! People everywhere are sold on the idea that if you wear the right outfit, spray on the best-smelling perfume, display the proper physique, and write the perfect profile, you will find love.

So, what is this "true love" that all people long for? One might first think of a romantic type of love. The love that is written about in most songs and novels is wonderful, but it is fleeting because it is based on human emotions and feelings. The type of love that humans truly desire is deeper than this. It is an unconditional love. It's a dependable love that never leaves you brokenhearted. Hear me when I say this, Sister, "YOU ARE LOVED!"

The greatest love story ever told was not written by Danielle Steele against the backdrop of Beverly Hills. The greatest love story ever written was penned by God. It began in Bethlehem and climaxed on a hill called Calvary. This love will never disappoint; it's an eternal, true love. It's "agape" love, the highest form of love. It's a love that is freely given to you by God and cannot be earned.

> The greatest love story ever told was not written by Danielle Steele against the backdrop of Beverly Hills. The greatest love story ever written was *penned by God.*

Romans 5:8 tells you that God loved you even while you were a sinner. You see, love isn't a feeling; it's an action verb! And God demonstrated His love for you by taking action. He sent His Son to earth as a sacrifice to guarantee that you can spend eternity with Him! Consequently, you can rely on His unconditional love in all circumstances for your entire life.

So today and every day moving forward, when you are in the midst of the madness and mayhem, sing out loud the lyrics to what is perhaps the greatest love song of all: "Jesus loves me this I know, for the Bible tells me so...." Remind yourself of the words from Jeremiah 31:3, "I have loved you with an everlasting love..." and then confidently claim, "**I am loved...because He said so!**"

Prayer

Dear Lord, What a relief it is to know that You love me, all of me, just the way I am. Thank You that I don't have to earn Your love. You proved Your love for me on Calvary with the sacrifice of Your son, Jesus. I love You with all my heart and I want to share Your love with all of those around me. In Jesus' name and for the Father's glory, Amen.

READ MORE

God's Word says you are loved...

Psalm 136:26 • Isaiah 54:10 • Jeremiah 31:3

John 15:9-10 • Romans 5:8 • 1 John 4:7-16

Do you believe that God loves you unconditionally (and that you don't have to keep trying to measure up to some unreachable standard)? **If so, how can this change the way you live every day, and how can you show your love to God and others?**

Daily Challenge:

#loved

- ❍ You are loved by an awesome God. Share the love today and send a text to remind someone that you love them and so does Jesus!

- ❍ Share a video, image, or your written testimony with other sisters in Christ in the "Because He Said So" Facebook group. Use the hashtag #loved and #iambecausehesaidso

Visit Facebook.com/groups/iambecausehesaidso to join the community!

Day 4

I am...
CHOSEN

"Therefore, as God's chosen people, holy and dearly loved, clothe yourselves with compassion, kindness, humility, gentleness and patience."

Colossians 3:12

Let's take a walk down memory lane, all the way back to your elementary school playground. Among the merry-go-rounds, slides, and monkey bars, imagine a group of kids. They are organizing the daily "game." Depending on the time of year, it could be football, kickball, softball, or even a game of Red Rover. Somewhere in the middle of this group are two "captains" who are picking their teams. One by one, kids are chosen to join a team; the most athletic kids are chosen quickly because of what they can offer the group. As the process continues, it becomes slower and slower as the talent pool becomes smaller and smaller. Finally, there are only a few kids left and the captains begrudgingly have to choose which least-talented classmates they will have on their team. For the kids left standing, this can be a grueling and embarrassing process because they feel they aren't good enough, talented enough, or liked enough to have their name called out.

Being chosen by Christ has *nothing* to do with your performance or how hard you have worked, but it has *everything* to do with Him and His grace!

You might have guessed by now that I am writing from experience. I was always one of the smallest girls in my class, and when combined with being a bit prissy and uncoordinated, I was seldom chosen before the last one or two picks of the teams. There were a few, very special occasions when one of my good friends was the captain and my name would be called early on in the process. Yes! It may have been a "pity pick", but...I didn't care. WHAT A GREAT FEELING IT WAS TO BE CHOSEN!

Perhaps your memories of not being chosen didn't exist on the playground, but somewhere else. Maybe you were wishing for someone special to choose you as his prom date. Perhaps it was a hope to be chosen as a member of a club. Or, it could have been a desire to be elected as Senior Class President. I am certain there has been a time in your life where you have felt the same longing to be chosen and disappointment when you were overlooked.

If you focus back on the present, being chosen still plays an important role in your life. You not only still long to be chosen, you work hard so that you will be offered the job, given the opportunity, or asked to participate and lead. And when you are not chosen, the feelings of inadequacy that you may have felt long ago while standing on that playground or sitting in a chair hoping to be asked to dance, can still come back and overwhelm you.

My sister, rejoice! You ARE chosen! You are chosen by the

Creator to be on His team, to work for Him, to participate in His purpose! Being chosen by Christ has nothing to do with your performance or how hard you have worked, but it has everything to do with Him and His grace! You do not have to earn a place on His roster. It is a position that's freely offered to you. He's calling your name and choosing you. All you have to do is accept Him as your captain and CEO. Deuteronomy 14:2 tells you that you are "set apart" and "chosen."

So today and every day moving forward, when life turns you down and you are overlooked, remember that God picked you and repeat these words, **"I am chosen...because He said so!"**

Prayer

Dear Lord, Please forgive me, for those times when I am preoccupied by being chosen by the world when You have already chosen me to be part of Your family. Thank You that Your choice wasn't based on what I could or couldn't do. I praise Your name that it wasn't based on anything but Your love for me. In Jesus' name and for the Father's glory, Amen.

READ MORE

God's Word says you are chosen...

Isaiah 43:10 • John 15:16

Galatians 1:15-16 • Ephesians 1:3-4 • 1 Peter 2:9

Do you realize how special you are because God has chosen you to be a part of his eternal family? Have you begun discovering what God has chosen *you* to do? **Will you write down what you believe God has chosen you to do and any action steps toward that call?**

Daily Challenge:

☐ Do you know someone who has recently been rejected? Encourage them by sharing the good news that they are hand-picked by God. Assure them that He will never turn His back on them.

☐ Share a video, image, or your written testimony with other sisters in Christ in the "Because He Said So" Facebook group. Use the hashtag #chosen and #iambecausehesaidso

Visit Facebook.com/groups/iambecausehesaidso to join the community!

Day 5

I am...
RESCUED

"I waited patiently for the Lord; he turned to me and heard my cry. He lifted me out of the slimy pit, out of the mud and mire; he set my feet on a rock and gave me a firm place to stand."

Psalm 40:1-2

Growing up, one of my favorite after-school TV Shows was "Gilligan's Island." You may be familiar with this iconic 70's sitcom that was the tale of seven stranded castaways who had set out on that infamous three-hour tour (yes, "a three-hour boat tour"). When "the weather started getting rough, the tiny ship was tossed" and crashed on an uncharted desert island. They were stranded in need of rescue. Episode after episode the characters were trying to find a way off that island. One airing showed one of the characters, "The Professor", trying to invent a contraption to send out an SOS. I had never heard of this before and later that night I asked my daddy about it. He explained to me that an SOS was a signal to let others know you needed to be rescued. I remember shouting, "Do you mean like yelling 'H-E-L-P!'?"

Unlike the fictitious friends from the SS Minnow, your rescue situation can be significantly less fun and entertaining. As a matter of fact, when you are truly in need of being rescued, the moments before help arrives can be excruciating, lonely, and filled with extreme fear and danger.

The Oxford Living Dictionary defines rescue as "to save from a dangerous or difficult situation." However, dictionary.com dives deeper into the meaning by defining it as "to free or deliver from confinement, violence, danger, or evil." It is in these types of situations when you truly need to send out an SOS!

> God promises to *never forsake* *us* in our time of weakness; so, rest assured that God sent Jesus to save us. He is the *Savior*.

You can't overlook the fact that there are people in the world who are in desperate need of rescue from serious, life-or-death situations which the majority of people cannot comprehend. Today, you may be in need of your own type of personal rescue. Perhaps you are crying for help to be freed from a stronghold, such as an addiction or fear. Maybe you are trying to escape a tumultuous relationship, overcome depression or thoughts of unworthiness and self-doubt. Maybe you need to be lifted out of the pool of drowning debt, thrown a lifeline to face another day after losing a loved one, or pulled out of the quicksand of sickness. Whatever your 9-1-1 situation is, do not hesitate to send up your prayers of SOS to your Heavenly Father. Claim Psalm 144:7, where David pleads with God, saying, "Reach down Your hand from on high; deliver me and rescue me from the mighty waters...."

God promises to never forsake you in your time of weakness; so, rest assured—that God sent Jesus to save you. He is the Savior. All you have to do is grab the gift of Christ; He is your life preserver! Whether it is immediately, progressively, or ultimately, you can be absolutely confident that He will rescue you in your desperation! The Prince of Peace came to pay your ransom, Sister, and He is mighty to save!

So today and every day moving forward, when you find yourself feeling distressed, send out an SOS to the Rescuer of your soul and claim, **"I am rescued...because He said so!"**

Prayer

Dear Lord, Thank You for rescuing me. Help me remember, Father, when I am facing a life or soul threatening situation, that You are the only SOS I need. You are my Savior and You will not leave me nor forsake me. I only need to turn to You. Use my survival story to show others that You and You alone are the Saver of Souls. In Jesus' name and for the Father's glory, Amen.

READ MORE

God's Word says you are rescued...

Psalm 18:18-19 • Psalm 34:17-18 • Psalm 145:18-19

Acts 2:21 • Galatians 1:3-5

Have you given your fears and strongholds to God yet? **If so, write about how you feel giving it to Him. Are you still feeling trapped by these circumstances, or are you living each day as someone who has already been rescued?**

Daily Challenge:

◯ Create Snack & Smile bags to help rescue the homeless. Keep in car to hand out as needed. (See Appendix 2 for more info and the directions on how to make these.)

◯ Share a video, image, or your written testimony with other sisters in Christ in the "Because He Said So" Facebook group. Use the hashtag #rescued and #iambecausehesaidso

Visit Facebook.com/groups/iambecausehesaidso to join the community!

Day 6

I am...
FORGIVEN

"In Him we have redemption through His blood, the forgiveness of our trespasses, according to the riches of His grace."

Ephesians 1:7

Not long after I had my second son, Morgan, my sweet younger sister, Amanda, was gracious enough to come and stay a few days to help me. One morning when Morgan was crying, and my postpartum hormones were raging, I snapped at her. All she was doing was trying to assist me and my new-born child, and I had acted ugly. As soon as the harsh words came out of my mouth, I saw the hurt on her face. I knew immediately that I had upset her, and I burst into tears. I told her I was wrong to speak to her like that. She said it was fine, but I kept apologizing...over and over again. After multiple apologies, Amanda kindly spoke to me the words I was longing to hear, "You don't have to keep asking, Sister, I forgive you."

Think about a time when you have let someone down, offended someone, or even caused emotional or physical pain by your words or actions. Whether the act was intentional, completely by accident, or like mine - fueled by postpartum depression, your actions led to someone else's hurt. The guilt often seems to be worse when you hurt someone whom you love and who loves you. You long to be back in their good graces, to be assured that your offense is forgiven. The thought of your act putting a wedge in your treasured relationship causes you to feel guilt and sadness. To make it right, you accept responsibility, apologize, and ask for forgiveness.

There is hope in the Savior that came to this world to take the sentence for your sin.

From the moment that darkness slithered into the garden, sin clashed with God here on earth. Sin separates you from your Heavenly Father; it puts a wedge in your relationship. Because He is a just God and hates sin, you must be punished for your wrongdoings. Roman 6:23 is a reminder that the wages of sin is death. But Sister, there is hope for your guilty soul! There is hope in the Savior that came to this world to take the sentence for your sin. Jesus went to the cross and bore the punishment of your offenses. He sacrificed His life so that you could live with God forever. Your Father loves you so much that He sent His only son to live on earth as a living sacrifice for you. This pardon is freely given and can't be earned. To receive this gift, all you have to do is confess your sins and lay them at the foot of the cross. And when you do this, you can know that your God is saying, "I forgive you."

So today and every day moving forward, when the evil one attempts to make you feel guilty and unworthy because of your past actions that seem unforgivable, get on your knees and thank your God for loving you so much that you can proclaim, **"I am forgiven...because He said so!"**

Prayer

Dear Lord, What a relief it is to know I am forgiven! The guilt from choices that I have made can be overwhelming and leave me feeling worthless and unworthy. I realize that there is nothing that I could ever do to earn Your forgiveness. It is only through the blood of Jesus I am forgiven. Thank you, Father, for Your love and Your mercy. In Jesus' name and for the Father's glory, Amen.

READ MORE

God's Word says you are forgiven...

Psalm 32:1-5 • Psalm 51:1-2 • Psalm 103:12

Matthew 18:21-22 • Ephesians 4:32 • 1 John 1:8-9

Do you feel condemned for all your past mistakes and failures? **1 John 1:9 tells you with certainty that if you confess your sins, He is faithful and just to forgive. What sins must you confess? How do you feel knowing you are forgiven?**

Daily Challenge:

#forgiven

☐ Who do you need to forgive for past wrongs or hurts? Pick up the phone and talk to them about how you want to put the past behind you. Offer them the same forgiveness that Christ offered you.

☐ Share a video, image, or your written testimony with other sisters in Christ in the "Because He Said So" Facebook group. Use the hashtag #forgiven and #iambecausehesaidso

Visit Facebook.com/groups/iambecausehesaidso to join the community!

Day 7

I am...
INNOCENT

"Their sins and their lawless deeds I will remember no more."

Hebrews 10:17

When all my to-dos are done, I love to turn on the television and relax. Recently, I have found myself looking for true crime TV shows like "Dateline", "Snapped", or "The First 48." I find them fascinating. All of these shows seem to follow the same general formula: they begin by painting a picture of the life of the characters before the crime, segue into the crime itself, and conclude with the verdict. Admittedly, once I begin watching one of these shows, I cannot tear myself away. I have to watch until the end. I must know if the accused is found guilty or innocent. I even watch for the updated information that is generally written in white text at the end of the show just before the credits. More often than not, when the verdict is read on these shows, we hear the word, "Guilty."

Have you ever imagined what it would be like to be the one on trial, standing accused of a horrific crime with an airtight case against you? All of the evidence presented is indisputable, and it is obvious to all that you are indeed guilty beyond a shadow of a doubt. The time comes for the reading of the verdict and, as the gavel falls, you hear the words, "I find the defendant...Not Guilty"! Everyone is stunned! What happened? How is this even possible? Where is the justice? This is not what you deserved!

Just remember that no sin is too much for His mercy.

Everyone should be prepared because one day each and every person will be on the docket to stand in front of The Great Judge. As a defendant, you should know that God is a just God; He cannot be bought, bribed, or bargained with. He hates sin, and Proverbs 11:19 clearly states that the pursuit of evil brings death. You should expect to be found guilty when the verdict is read because you, along with all the other people in this world, are flawed. It is impossible for you to live a perfect life and to keep the entire law that God established. James 2:10 clearly states, "For whoever keeps the whole law but fails in one point has become accountable for all of it."

Someone has to pay the price for your sin. As touched on yesterday, all humans are sinners, but, as a Christian, you are also forgiven. The amazing fact is, your precious Savior went beyond simply forgiving you. You no longer have to try to cover your sins with fig leaves like Adam and Eve or with animal sacrifices as was required by Jewish law. This is because the sacrifice of Jesus has removed your sins and God remembers them no more! You are guilty but declared innocent through the sacrifice of Christ. He paid a great price indeed for your innocence. But be on your guard: There is nothing the enemy would love more than for you to let your guilt rob you of this priceless gift. You see, guilt creates shame and separation from your Father. Remember that no sin is too much for His mercy; it doesn't matter what you've done. It matters what Jesus did. He took the sentence that was meant for you. Because of this, God won't hold your sin against you anymore. There is no reason to keep feeling guilty about it.

When you accept the gift of Jesus, delivered to you first in the form of a baby, sent to earth to live and ultimately die as a sacrifice for your sin, you are not just forgiven, but the slate of your life is wiped clean. God now sees you as blameless.

So today and every day moving forward, when you replay the recording of all of your hurts, habits, and hang-ups, don't let the devil steal what was divinely given to you. Believe what God's word clearly states. Stop slouching with condemnation and stand tall and shout, **"I am innocent...because He said so!"**

Prayer

Dear Lord, When I feel bad about all the mistakes I have made throughout my life, remind me that, because of the cross, You have separated me from my sins as far as the east is from the west. You have declared me innocent by the blood of the Lamb. Thank You for the fact that because of Jesus, You see me as blameless. In Jesus' name and for the Father's glory, Amen.

READ MORE

God's Word says you are innocent...

Psalm 19:12-13 ● Psalm 51:5-7 ● Isaiah 1:18

Romans 8:1 ● Jude 1:24

Does knowing that God sees you as "innocent" change the way you see yourself? **In what ways does this alter the way you live your life?**

Daily Challenge:

- ☐ Find a picture of yourself as a baby. Put in a prominent place. Use this image to remind you that, because of Jesus, God sees you as innocent as any beautiful newborn baby.

- ☐ Share a video, image, or your written testimony with other sisters in Christ in the "Because He Said So" Facebook group. Use the hashtag #innocent and #iambecausehesaidso

Visit Facebook.com/groups/iambecausehesaidso to join the community!

Day 8

I am...
REDEEMED

"I have swept away your offenses like a cloud, your sins like the morning mist. Return to me, for I have redeemed you."

Isaiah 44:22

I've tried; I really have. But I just haven't mastered the art of couponing. It is a brilliant idea, isn't it? Businesses give us these vouchers that can be traded in or exchanged for something of much greater cost. We can turn in a piece of paper for incredible savings on their product. Combined over time, these little slips of paper can accumulate a great value in savings. Back in the day, coupons were available only from printed publications like newspapers and magazines. Now, these tokens of savings are found with a click of a mouse. There are websites and apps that can search for savings on a particular product or item and, with a swipe on our phone, we can redeem a deal. There was even a television series about couponing, "Extreme Couponing", where contestants competed to see who could save the most money while on a shopping spree. A savvy "couponer" could bring the total due down to zero!

During this journey, you have learned that God has forgiven you, and that you are innocent because of Christ. But God loves you so much that He doesn't stop there. In the currency of Christ, you can trade in your mistakes for His mercy and your failures for His forgiveness. With His sacrifice, your sins and shame are swiped away. What was once a blot on your record becomes a beautiful recount of God's narrative of your life. Through the blood of Christ, you are redeemed. Unlike the menial coupons that can be redeem for savings on common household products, this sacrifice was significant: Jesus gave His life to take your ugly past and make it beautiful. It's difficult to comprehend isn't it? God loved you so much that He sent Christ to die, so that you could live a blameless and beautiful life? Yes, yes He did! There are stories all through the Bible where you can see that this is true. For example, Paul committed grievous acts against the early Christians and, despite all of the horrible things he did, God forgave him and found him innocent. Through God's grace Paul, a murderer, became a messenger. God takes people whose lives are dark and worthless and redeems them for something of greater value. He makes the ugly pretty. He makes the disgraceful good. He makes the foul forgiven.

> In the currency of Christ, we can trade in our mistakes for His *mercy* and our failures for His *forgiveness*.

Sister, you are wiped clean with a zero balance—nothing left to pay—because Jesus paid it all. He exchanged His life for yours. You are an imperfect person loved by a perfect God. "He makes beauty out of ashes" (Isaiah 61:3).

So today and every day moving forward, when you feel the guilt and see the grime of your past, remember that you have been bathed in the blood of Christ and made totally clean. Look in the mirror remembering His grace and recite these words, "**I am redeemed…because He said so!**"

Prayer

Dear Lord, Let me never forget that You traded the perfect life of Jesus for my mistake and sin filled life so that I could be one with You. In the process, You redeemed me into something valuable - Your child. I am overwhelmed and so thankful that because of Jesus' sacrifice my life is now worthy of Your love and forgiveness. In Jesus' name and for the Father's glory, Amen.

READ MORE

God's Word says you are redeemed...

Psalm 103:1-4 • Isaiah 43:1-2 • Galatians 3:13-14

Titus 2:14 • 1 Peter 1:18-19

Are you thanking Jesus daily for trading His life for yours and saving you? **Since God has redeemed you, what ways do you express that redemption in your everyday life?**

Daily Challenge:

#redeemed

○ Using red lipstick, write on your mirror "I am redeemed" and remember God is making something beautiful with your life. Let the color of the lipstick remind you that this is possible because of His blood.

○ Share a video, image, or your written testimony with other sisters in Christ in the "Because He Said So" Facebook group. Use the hashtag #redeemed and #iambecausehesaidso

Visit Facebook.com/groups/iambecausehesaidso to join the community!

Day 9

I am...
TRANSFORMED

"Do not conform to the pattern of this world but be transformed by the renewing of your mind. Then you will be able to test and approve what God's will is, his good, pleasing and perfect will."

Romans 12:2

Whether it is learning how to win friends and influence people, become more fit, control emotions, get rich, find a meaningful relationship, communicate more effectively, or become a better leader, people want to experience transformation. The personal development industry is evidence of that with all its books, podcasts, webinars, workshops and seminars. Consequently, "self-help" has become an 11-billion-dollar market and is on the rise because people desperately want to change. Don't get me wrong, I happen to enjoy reading books and attending conferences that equip me with ideas of ways to be a better version of myself. I love absorbing knowledge on how to more effectively provide value to people and to not just communicate, but to connect with them. I work for one of the foremost authorities in the field, Dr. John C Maxwell. As a life coach, I consult with people every day who are craving transformation in their lives. I have a true passion for helping people connect the dots between their passion and their purpose.

There isn't a need to search high and low for the newest best seller to find the answer to living a transformed life; it's right in front of you. The answer can be found in the number one best-selling book of all time, The Good Book - The Bible! All the instructions that you ever need to experience true transformation are right there in God's written words to you. When you spend time in the presence of God, and let His words pour into you as you read, you experience a renewing of your mind and spirit. Experiencing life-transformation begins with accepting the sacrifice of Jesus and allowing the Holy Spirit into your deepest self to make you new and to guide your decisions. True transformation is about more than plugging a new strategy into your morning routine or changing an item on your daily to-do list. True transformation requires a change in your heart and mind. It's about putting Christ first, others next, and self last. It's not about growing yourself more; it's about giving more of yourself. It's about confessing your sins and your need for a Savior to rescue you from them. It also means abandoning your old ways of thinking about yourself. In 2 Corinthians 5:17, you are reminded, "Therefore, if anyone is in Christ, he is a new creation. The old has passed away; behold, the new has come."

> True transformation requires a change in our *heart and mind.*

Like a blob of clay that the potter throws on his wheel, may you allow God to mold your life to His will. May He transform your blob into a beautiful vessel for Him. "Because of the Lord's great love, we are not consumed, for his compassions never fail. They are new every morning; great is your faithfulness" (Lamentations 3:22-23). Sister, my prayer is that you will not only experience true transformation but thirst for it daily. I pray you will wake up every morning feeling different than you did the day before. It is my prayer that you will seek every day to grow closer to God by focusing on Him more and yourself less. My hope is that the transformation you experience will be so profound that you actually start to look and act more like Jesus.

So today and every day moving forward, when you look in the mirror remind yourself that by trusting God now, you won't be the same tomorrow. And, because of the work of The Potter's hand, you can proudly proclaim, **"I am transformed...because He said so!"**

Prayer

Dear Lord, Thank You for transforming me. I now have a new self—one with You at its core. Help me to continue to transform my life, my thoughts, my words, and my deeds a little more each day to line up with Your word. I want the transformation in my life to be so obvious that when people see me, they see You! In Jesus' name and for the Father's glory, Amen.

READ MORE

God's Word says you are transformed...

Isaiah 42:9 • Jeremiah 18:6 • Ezekiel 36:26-27

Romans 8:6 • Romans 12:2 • Revelation 21:5

In the chaos of your busy day, are you taking moments of time to renew your mind so that it lines up with God's word? **In what ways do you want God to transform you? How can you use that transformation to serve Him?**

Daily Challenge:

#transformed

- ☐ Sketch two pictures today: a caterpillar and a butterfly. Think about the miraculous transformation that occurs and ask God to transform your life into something marvelous, too.

- ☐ Share a video, image, or your written testimony with other sisters in Christ in the "Because He Said So" Facebook group. Use the hashtag #transformed and #iambecausehesaidso

Visit Facebook.com/groups/iambecausehesaidso to join the community!

Day 10

I am...
FREE

"If the Son sets you free, you will be free indeed."

John 8:36

Growing up I always had an earlier curfew than any of my friends. My daddy was really over-protective, and he wanted me home early. In actuality, he would have preferred that I not go out at all. He liked his chickens in their nest. When my friends and I had big plans for our weekend, which generally included cruising around Cloverleaf Mall, I stayed at someone else's home, where there was a little more freedom. Going into my senior year I decided to ask my daddy to extend my curfew to midnight. I was nervous about the conversation, but, one night at dinner, I posed the question. With tears in his eyes, he removed the restrictions of a curfew altogether, asking only that I let my mother and him know where I was going to be, whom I was going to be with, and what time to expect me home. WOW! I felt such freedom in that. I felt like such a "grown up" when I told my friends that I didn't have a curfew. Finally, the taste of freedom!

Freedom means different things at different stages of life. When you were a toddler, you wanted to be free from your parents' laps to roam and explore. As a teenager you want to be free to come and go with your friends without the restraints of a curfew. As you enter adulthood, you wanted to be free from being dependent on your parents as you strived to "make it on your own." And, as you grow older, you want to be free from debt, stress, and the demands of this world.

You came into this world as a sinner and, from the beginning, you were under condemnation. Yet, miraculously, even though you were a sinner, Christ gave His life for you. His gift of grace is the ransom that sets you free. "For the wages of sin is death, but the gift of God is eternal life in Christ Jesus our Lord." (Romans 6:23). Satan may try to use your transgressions to rob you of your freedom. He may relentlessly accuse you, so that you feel enslaved to your mistakes, captive to your strongholds, and hostage to your sins. You may feel guilt, shame, and condemnation. These sins could possibly become the chains that weigh you down. You might literally keep yourself a prisoner of your past. But Christ sets you free from the shackles of sin. He releases you from the bondage of shame. And as the spotlight scripture says, "Whom the Son has set free is free indeed!" So why then do you allow your sins to keep you in the slammer? You are free, and you need to live like you are free!

> Freedom means *fearless living.* It means doing crazy things just because our Heavenly Father *calls* us to do them.

Freedom in Christ means that you are unrestricted to be all that you were created to be. It means fearless living. It means doing crazy things just because your Heavenly Father calls you to do them—like boldly sharing personal stories of pain or abuse because the experiences will help someone else. It means telling your tale of brokenness to the broken. It means writing the tough story or song about God's rescue and deliverance. It means reaching out to someone when you receive that prompting from the Spirit even if you don't feel like it. It means living boldly! 2 Corinthians 3:12 reminds us, "Therefore, since we have such a hope, we are very bold."

God tells Moses in Exodus 7:16, "Then say to him [Pharaoh], 'The LORD, the God of the Hebrews, has sent me to say to you: Let my people go, so that they may worship me in the wilderness.'" My sweet sister, you are free; free to worship Him and live out your purpose! Run toward your calling like a racehorse right out of the starting gate!

So today and every day moving forward, when it feels like you are imprisoned by your imperfections and restrained by your regrets, lift your hands in praise and proclaim, "**I am free...because He said so!**"

Prayer

Dear Lord, Forgive me for those times that I listen to Satan. He loves to remind me of bad habits that I haven't broken or weaknesses I still have. Remind me that there is freedom in Jesus. Show me how to "live free" every day and in every aspect of my life so others will want to experience the true freedom that I have found in You. In Jesus' name and for the Father's glory, Amen.

READ MORE

God's Word says you are free...

Psalm 142:7 • Isaiah 52:1-2 • 2 Corinthians 3:17

Galatians 5:1 • Ephesians 3:12

Do you believe deep in your heart that you are free in Christ? **If you were to actually live in the freedom that Christ has given you, what would you do that you haven't done yet?**

Daily Challenge:

◯ Download the song "Chain Breaker" by Zach Williams. Listen to it anytime you need to be reminded that you are free from the chains of sin and shame. Praise and give thanks to Jesus.

◯ Share a video, image, or your written testimony with other sisters in Christ in the "Because He Said So" Facebook group. Use the hashtag #free and #iambecausehesaidso

Visit Facebook.com/groups/iambecausehesaidso to join the community!

Day 11

I am...
HEALED

"Heal me, Lord, and I will be healed; save me and I will be saved, for you are the one I praise."

Jeremiah 17:14

It was early on February 21,1987 when Dr. Varner, a personal friend of the family, came into the cold grey room where we were gathered. Through tears, he spoke these 6 words: "I'm sorry; he didn't make it." Wait, what? He didn't make it? He had just become sick the day before, and the surgery was successful. No! This didn't make sense; it was hard to comprehend. My daddy, only 42 years old, was gone! My heart ached, and my blood boiled. Why would God allow this? Why hadn't God healed my daddy?

There is evidence of Jesus healing and performing miracles throughout the Gospels. He healed many sick and afflicted people: a paralyzed man, a leper, a blind man, a deaf man, and a bleeding woman just to name a few. He even raised people from the dead. Talk about healing! When you think about healing, your thoughts generally go directly to physical healing. But there is so much more to the word "heal." Therefore, it is important to look a little deeper.

The Hebrew word for heal is "Rapha"; it simply means to make thoroughly whole. If that's the case…isn't everyone in need of healing? No one is thoroughly whole. Even if you are blessed at the current time to be physically healthy, you have wounds that haven't mended; you are all looking to be made whole. The cure to your unhealthy life can't be found in a medicine bottle, prescribed pill, or a home remedy. Please don't think that I am suggesting that you don't need to seek the advice/treatment of physicians or that you should throw out your medications and supplements used for treating your illnesses and/or health conditions. I'm not. I am, however, recommending a big dose of Jesus! It is by His stripes you are healed. It is because of His death your disease is defeated! It is through His sacrifice your sickness subsides. As a result of His wounds, you are made well. When you are in Him your prognosis is certain. You have a 100% survival rate. You may be like the bleeding woman and healed instantly, or you may be healed, like my daddy, ultimately! Rest assured, you will be healed. You will be made thoroughly whole for eternity.

> The Hebrew word for heal is "Rapha"; It simply means to make *thoroughly whole*.

You may be suffering from a physical or emotional illness or a disease that is causing you pain and/or threatening your quality of life, indeed your very life. You may be agonizing over a wounded relationship. You might be aching with the grief of a loss. You may be experiencing the sting of sin and shame caused by sin. You may be hurting, but, my sister, you can celebrate today because no matter your situation, you are healed! Praise the Lord! Your

God is still in the miracle business! "But he was pierced for our transgressions, he was crushed for our iniquities; the punishment that brought us peace was on him, and by his wounds we are healed" (Isaiah 53:5).

So today and every day moving forward, when the wounds become tender and the pain is pronounced, place your hand on your heart and proclaim, **"I am healed...because He said so!"**

Prayer

Dear Lord, Forgive me when I forget that you are my Healer. Remind me that any pain, physical or emotional, that I experience here on earth is only temporary. Because of Jesus' stripes I am completely healed for eternity. Thank You for my healing that only comes from You as You are the God who heals! In Jesus' name and for the Father's glory, Amen.

READ MORE

God's Word says you are healed...

Exodus 15:26 • Psalm 107:19-20 • Psalm 147:3

Psalm 30:2 • Malachi 4:2 • 1 Peter 2:24

Do you struggle with praising God while you are sick or in pain? **What do you need God to heal you from? How does knowing that ultimate healing is yours help you through the pain of today?**

Daily Challenge:

#healed

☐ Send a card to someone who is sick or in need of healing. Reference today's verse in your note to encourage them and remind them that Jesus is the cure.

☐ Share a video, image, or your written testimony with other sisters in Christ in the "Because He Said So" Facebook group. Please use the hashtags #healed and #iambecausehesaidso on all social media posts.

Visit Facebook.com/groups/iambecausehesaidso to join the community!

Day 12

I am...
ALIVE

"But because of his great love for us, God, who is rich in mercy, made us alive with Christ, even when we were dead in our trespasses. It is by grace you have been saved."

Ephesians 2:4-5

In the 1980s Dunkin Donuts came out with a commercial that lends itself beautifully to our topic today. The advertisement began with a chubby middle-aged man, Fred the Baker, aka the "Time to Make the Donuts" guy, turning off his alarm clock before dawn. As he leaves his house, he grabs his hat and shuffles out the door saying, "Time to make the donuts!" In the next scene we see Fred returning home at day's end saying, "I made the donuts!" This repeats many times over during the 30-second ad until Fred meets himself coming and going. Funny as it is, I believe that we behave much like the "Time to Make the Donuts" Guy. We are taking the same steps day after day after day. We "schedule in" our quiet time and prayer time with hopes of wrapping it up in timely manner so that we aren't running late for work or in hopes that we can get in bed a little earlier. We say the same prayers, in the same way, day after day. And we are happy with these habits; they are comfortable! I have to ask you, my sister in Christ, has your routine become a rut?

Today I want to encourage you to step out of your comfort zone and to break the hypnosis of the humdrum. "This is why it is said: 'Wake up, sleeper, rise from the dead, and Christ will shine on you'" (Ephesians 5:14). You need to stop doing the same old things in the same old ways you've always done them. Over the last few days you have discovered that you are forgiven, innocent, and free. You've claimed the promises of God and celebrated the fact that you are a new creation in Him being transformed daily. You heard the words, "you are healed"! So, why then would you live the same ordinary "Time to Make the Donuts" kind of life? I don't know about you, but I think my new life in Christ is exciting! It gives me a skip in my step! And I don't want to sluggishly shuffle through my schedule anymore. I want to be vibrant and alive and full of Christ and His light! The only way to accomplish this is to let go of the muck of the mundane and to depend on Him with a childlike trust to find the joy and peace that only He can give.

Wake up, sleeper, rise from the dead, and Christ will shine on you!

These questions remain: Do you believe that you are created to be fully alive in Christ? Are you willing to step outside your comfort zone and do things that you've never done in ways you've never done them? Are you willing to let His light shine through you in ways you have possibly never even imagined? It's time to strive to have a relationship with Him and do life with Him in ways that go beyond your "scheduled" quiet time each day. It's time to step out of your comfort zone. I mean, after all, isn't that what this study is all about? It's about changing your thoughts and your words and to truly begin believing that He has called you to live more fully in Him. Routines can become ruts...even in your prayer life and relationship with God.

So today and every day moving forward, when you need to shake up your faith journey a bit, make a plan to make the most of every minute. And declare in Christ's name, **"I am alive...because He said so!"**

Prayer

Dear Lord, I am so sorry. I didn't realize that I have been just "going through the motions" in some areas of my life - even in my relationship with You! Please forgive me. I am excited about Your life in me. I am thankful for all the blessings you've given me. Show me how to make the most of every moment so that others want to be alive in You. In Jesus' name and for the Father's glory, Amen.

READ MORE

God's Word says you are alive...

Proverbs 18:21 • John 10:10 • Romans 6:8-11

Romans 8:10-11 • Ephesians 5:14-16 • Colossians 2:13

Has the "routine" of your daily life put your spiritual life in a rut? **What can you do today to shake things up a bit and truly be alive in Christ?**

Daily Challenge:

- ☐ Write out John 3:16 on an index card. If you don't know this verse by heart, memorize it. If you do, pass the card on to someone who may need these life affirming words!

- ☐ Share a video, image, or your written testimony with other sisters in Christ in the "Because He Said So" Facebook group. Please use the hashtags #alive and #iambecausehesaidso on all social media posts.

Visit Facebook.com/groups/iambecausehesaidso to join the community!

Day 13

I am...
APPROVED

> *"But just as we have been approved by God to be entrusted with the gospel, so we speak, not as pleasing men, but God who examines our hearts."*
>
> **1 Thessalonians 2:4**

My name is Missy, and I am a people pleaser. There, I said it! Isn't that the first step to recovery? Indeed, it is; the first step to recovery is awareness and acknowledgment that there is a problem. And, Houston…we have a problem. Even as I write these words, I am fighting my thoughts of hoping that you "approve" of these written words you are reading.

Perhaps I can trace this addiction back to my early years. I am the daughter of a mom who was physically abused by her husband, my biological father. Although God rescued us from that situation when my mom divorced him, somewhere deep down in my little 4-year old soul, I felt it was my responsibility to make sure she was happy. I wanted to be the perfect daughter and do things that made her smile. Without a doubt, the feeling that we receive when someone approves of us and accepts us is as addictive as any drug.

I'm a big girl now, but I still struggle with longing for the approval of others. I want so badly to be liked, to fit in, to be seen as worthy in the eyes of others. This is a stronghold in my life, a sin I struggle with and one that the enemy loves to use against me. But I am learning to give this struggle to God. I surrender it to Him on a daily basis. In the Good News Translation of Proverbs 29:25 we read, "It is dangerous to be concerned with what others think of you, but if you trust the LORD, you are safe." I no longer want to be controlled by the opinions of others. I'm tired of saying yes, just because I am afraid of saying no. I want to be free of the fetters of human approval. I only want to please Him. My heart's desire is to live out Matthew 6:33, seeking first the kingdom of God and His righteousness!

> You are approved by God not by what you *do* that pleases Him, but by your *faith in Him*.

Genesis is the story of creation. During those six days God created the heavens and the earth; the sky and the land; the water and the plants; the stars, sun, and moon; and all of the creatures. With each creation, He declared it was good. But He saved the best for last — mankind. When He made man He proclaimed, "It is very good!" He put His seal of approval on you when He created human life! He doesn't approve of you because of what you do; He approves of you because of what Jesus did! In Genesis 15:6, you see that Abraham was approved by God not for his acts or for adhering to the law, but for his faith. Romans 4:22-24 reads, "*This is why 'it was credited to him as righteousness.' The words 'it was credited to him' were not written only for Abraham, but also for us, to whom God will credit righteousness — for us who believe in him who raised Jesus our Lord from the dead.*" In these verses you see that the promise to

Abraham is also a promise to you. You are approved by God not by what you "do" that pleases Him, but by your faith in Him.

Jesus didn't need to please men because He already had God's approval. Sister, you don't need anyone else's approval either — because when you repent of your sins and accept Christ's sacrifice on the cross, God's approval is yours. And one day, you will stand in front of your Heavenly Father and hear the words, "Well done, my good and faithful servant! This is my daughter with whom I am well pleased!"

So today and every day moving forward, when you feel rejected by family or friends, invalidated by your boss, or unwanted by the world, lift your arms up to your Abba Father and claim, "**I am approved...because He said so!**"

Prayer

Dear Lord, Forgive me for running around trying to get approval from others. Thank You for reminding me that I don't need it. I already have Your approval, which You gave me through Jesus Christ, My Savior and Lord. YOU are my validation, the proof of my worth and worthiness. I can stand tall because You approve of me. Thank You. In Jesus' name and for the Father's glory, Amen.

READ MORE

God's Word says you are approved...

Genesis 1:31 • Romans 14:18 • 2 Corinthians 10:18

Galatians 1:10 • Hebrews 11:2 • 2 Timothy 2:15

If you are being honest with yourself, are you seeking approval from someone other than God? **What can you do to re-set your focus on the Lord?**

Daily Challenge:

#approved

◯ Write "Approved by God" on a sticky note(s) and place in various common areas around your home and work to remind yourself that His approval is the only approval that you need.

◯ Share a video, image, or your written testimony with other sisters in Christ in the "Because He Said So" Facebook group. Please use the hashtags #approved and #iambecausehesaidso on all social media posts.

Visit Facebook.com/groups/iambecausehesaidso to join the community!

Day 14

I am...
ACCEPTED

"To the praise of the glory of his grace, wherein he hath made us accepted in the beloved."

Ephesians 1:6 (KJV)

My youngest son, Morgan, has wanted to be a doctor since he was a little boy. Now, as I am writing this, he is a college student pursuing his dream. It won't be easy. He will have to work hard to prove himself worthy. He will have to graduate college with a near perfect GPA. He will have to score high on the MCAT. He will have to complete applications, submit entrance essays, and endure a series of interviews. And then, he will have to wait. Morgan's acceptance into medical school is not guaranteed despite his hard work or performance. His fate will be in the hands of a medical school admissions board. Will he be rejected, wait-listed, or accepted?

Being accepted can span from big, seemingly important life-altering things, like medical school, law school, or advanced degree programs, etc.; to a family or friend group; to a club, social group, or organization; or to something as absolutely trivial as a friend request on Facebook. No matter what it is, big or small, everyone wants to be accepted. There is an inherent human desire to belong. People work hard to prove themselves and meet the expectations of those around them so that they will be accepted.

Is there a sweeter illustration of your acceptance by God than the thief on the cross? At the time of Jesus' crucifixion, there were two other men, both thieves, also being executed. The thieves and many of the spectators were mocking and criticizing Jesus. In the midst of this Jesus cried out, "Father, forgive them, they know not what they do" (Luke 23:34). One thief was moved, convicted in his heart, that Jesus was indeed the Messiah. This penitent thief changed his tune and started defending Jesus. He told the other thief that Jesus had committed no crime and that they were the ones who deserved punishment. He then, with faith, turned to Jesus recognizing Him as King and said, "Jesus, remember me when you come into your kingdom" (Luke 23:42). And what did Jesus do? He accepted him on the spot. No applications to complete, no interview to go through—just a heart convicted, and a faith pronounced. Jesus said to him, "Truly I tell you, today you will be with Me in Paradise" (Luke 23:43).

Is there a sweeter illustration of our acceptance by God than the thief on the cross?

Because of Christ, you meet every requirement to be accepted into eternity with God. God doesn't see your crimes. He sees the crimson blood of Christ covering you, and you are made innocent. But I can't let this devotion come to an end without asking...have YOU accepted this gift? Have you said, "Lord, I recognize you as my Savior, and I surrender my life to you?" If not, why wait another minute? There's freedom at the cross! Perhaps this is hard to believe; you may wonder how it can be that easy. You may have worked your entire life to be accepted by others and find yourself repeatedly rejected. Do not despair! If you've never felt like you were fully accepted, even by your own parents, your Heavenly Father will welcome you with open arms! "Though my father and mother forsake me, the Lord will receive me" (Psalm 27:10).

My sweet sister, there is cause for celebration today! You are accepted into God's family! All you have to do is RSVP—just accept His invitation, and He will welcome you. Be comforted to know that you don't have to work your way into the Kingdom of God. Jesus already paid the price for your admission. No waiting list for you…you are accepted!

So today and every day moving forward, when you're feeling weary from working to be accepted in the world, wake up and walk to the mirror proclaiming, "**I am accepted…because He said so!**"

Prayer

Dear Lord, What a relief it is to know that I am accepted by You - into Your family, into an eternal relationship with You. It doesn't matter that people may have rejected me during my life. They don't control my future—You do! Jesus paid my way. I am so grateful, God, for Your love and for accepting me. In Jesus' name and for the Father's glory, Amen.

READ MORE

God's Word says you are accepted...

Psalm 19:14 • John 3:16 • Romans 5:8

Romans 15:7 • 1 Peter 2:5

Have you spent time trying to be accepted by other people? **Think about why the acceptance of others is so important to you. How will knowing that you are already accepted by God change the way you seek to be accepted by the world?**

Daily Challenge:

#accepted

☐ God's acceptance is unconditional when we acknowledge Him as our savior. See Appendix 3 for a simple prayer that you can say to invite Him into your heart or to praise Him for this gift you already have.

☐ Share a video, image, or your written testimony with other sisters in Christ in the "Because He Said So" Facebook group. Please use the hashtags #accepted and #iambecausehesaidso on all social media posts.

Visit Facebook.com/groups/iambecausehesaidso to join the community!

Day 15

I am...

INVITED

> *"Come to me, all you who are weary and burdened, and I will give you rest."*
>
> ***Matthew 11:28***

Everyone wants to be on the guest list. Whether we are asked to grab a coffee with a co-worker, invited to "do lunch" with a girlfriend, called to join our neighbors for a dinner, made the list for a Super Bowl Party, or included in a "special invitation only" event, it feels nice to be asked, invited, included.

In sixth grade, the new girl at school was having a party, and I so hoped I would be included. I went to the mailbox every day checking to see if my invitation had arrived, and day after day, I was met with disappointment. I never received an invitation, and the party came and went without me. Ironically, the Monday after the party, there was a torn and tattered invitation that had apparently been lost in the mail. I had been asked to attend the party, but I missed out because I didn't receive the invitation; I didn't know I was invited.

Sister, do not miss this invitation! God is cordially inviting you to "do life" with Him...for eternity! And He goes beyond simply extending the offer; He is beckoning you, calling you, pleading with you! "On the last and greatest day of the festival, Jesus stood and said in a loud voice, "Let anyone who is thirsty come to me and drink" (John 7:37). In this passage, Jesus is shouting to the crowd inviting them to join Him. In your life, Jesus often encourages you to join Him—not with a shout—but with a whisper. His invitations are delivered through His Word and through the Holy Spirit. "Softly and tenderly, Jesus is calling, calling for you and for me". Can you hear Him?

One of the images that comes to mind when I think of being invited to live with Christ is the image of the last supper. In Matthew 26:26-30 we see Jesus at the table with His friends, His disciples. He invites them to eat the bread and drink from the cup that represent His body and His blood that would be sacrificed for them. He offers that to you today; all you have to do is confess, repent, and accept Him as your Lord and Savior. At His table you will no longer thirst, you will no longer be hungry, and you will find rest for your weary soul.

> Our Heavenly Father invites you to be in fellowship with Him *now and forever.*

Our Heavenly Father invites you to be in fellowship with Him now and forever. He is waiting for you with open arms. All you have to do is accept his call. This is a "come as you are" invitation for eternity. You can never wear out your welcome with Him.

So today and every day moving forward, when you need to pack up your problems, bring your burdens, and show up with your sins in response to His call. He has you covered! Rejoice in thanksgiving and praise as you say, "**I am invited...because He said so!**" And...if you have never accepted His call, I pray that you will follow up God's invitation with... "**I accept!**"

Prayer

Dear Lord, Thank You for Your invitation. To have been invited to have a relationship with You now and for eternity is the greatest blessing of my life. I'm so glad that I said yes. Lord, I ask for You to give me opportunities to share Your invitation with others, so they don't miss out on all that You have planned for them. In Jesus' name and for the Father's glory, Amen.

READ MORE

God's Word says you are invited...

Psalm 66:5   Isaiah 55:1-3   Matthew 19:14-15

John 3:16   Revelation 3:20   Revelation 22:17

God will fill your life with overflowing joy and peace. Have you said yes to His invitation, to Jesus as your personal Savior and Lord? **If no is your answer, what is holding you back? If you have already accepted His invitation, how has this changed your life? With whom can you share this invitation?**

Daily Challenge:

- ☐ Who do you know that needs to claim their true identity in Christ? Ask ladies in your life to go on this journey with you. Invite them to the "Because He Said So" Facebook Community.

- ☐ Share a video, image, or your written testimony with other sisters in Christ in the "Because He Said So" Facebook group. Please use the hashtags #invited and #iambecausehesaidso on all social media posts.

Visit Facebook.com/groups/iambecausehesaidso to join the community!

Day 16

I am a...
PRINCESS

"So, in Christ Jesus you are all children of God through faith."

Galatians 3:26

For my generation, it began with Diana Frances Spencer. The world became obsessed with her beauty, her style, her grace! Many of us woke up in the middle of the night to watch her, a commoner, step out of her royal carriage, walk down the aisle, exchange vows with Prince Charles, and "become" royalty— become Princess Diana! The world's preoccupation with royalty has only become more frenzied since the untimely death of the beloved Princess Diana. The two newest princesses of the family, Kate and Megan are now the subject of the world's fixation. Everything they do, good and bad, is reported by the tabloids. If they eat too much pasta, the media proclaims, "a royal baby is on the way". These ladies are put on a pedestal and not only celebrated but also scrutinized. Let's not forget that because they represent the royal family, if the mistake they make is severe enough they may very well be disinherited.

When I was a little girl I would put on my mom's high heels, clip a pair of sparkling plastic jewels to my ears, drape a towel over my head and top it with a plastic crown. I walked slowly down our hallway toward my imaginary prince, and I married him. Then, I used the wand from my magic kit as my scepter, sat in my daddy's big chair, and waved to my subjects like only royalty can. I was Princess Missy. I would imagine that most little girls at some time in their lives dream of having Prince Charming ride in on his white horse and sweep them off their feet. They dream of a tiara being placed on their head and a title placed in front of their name: Princess _____. Oh, to be a part of the royal family!

> Listen, my sisters, has God not chosen those who are poor in the world to be rich in faith and *heirs of the kingdom*, which he has promised to those who *love* him?

In Revelation 19:16, the scriptures proclaim that God is the King of kings and Lord of lords. When you were made new in Christ, you were also adopted by the King! Tell me: What rank does the daughter of a king hold? Yes! The daughter of a king is a princess. And because you were adopted, purchased by the blood of Jesus into the royal family of God, you are a princess! So why then, do you live like a commoner? You allow the enemy (Satan) to cause you to doubt your birthright! You bow down to the world thinking you aren't worthy of your title. Sister, always remember this—no matter how bad things seem to get: Through Christ you are the child of the King! God will never disinherit you!

Being a part of THE Royal Family is about more than pearly gates, streets of gold, jeweled crowns, and magnificent mansions. You are representing your Heavenly Father, the King, here on earth. When people see you, you want to reflect Him! You want to be His hands and His feet to the people who are in need of Him.

Oh, how much better your "happily ever after" is in this tale! "Listen, my beloved brothers [and sisters], has not God chosen those who are poor in the world to be rich in faith and heirs of the kingdom, which he has promised to those who love him?" (James 2:5). With God as your Father, you are covered in the robe of righteousness and will walk the streets of gold with Him, the King, for eternity.

So today and every day moving forward, when you feel like Cinderella after the stroke of midnight crying next to a rotting pumpkin with only one glass slipper on. Stand up with the dignity and confidence of a royal. Straighten your crown, praise your Father, the King, and proclaim, **"I am a princess...because He said so!"**

Prayer

Dear Lord, Even when the world wants me to believe that I am worthless and a nobody, I know that I am special in Your eyes. You have declared that I am Your child, Your adopted daughter, and a joint heir with Christ. I praise You Abba, my Father and King, for bringing me into Your royal family. In Jesus' name and for the Father's glory, Amen.

READ MORE

God's Word says you are a princess...

2 Samuel 7:14 ● John 1:12 ● Romans 8:16-17

Ephesians 1:5 ● Ephesians 2:4-7 ● 1 John 3:1

Do you get distracted by your problems and forget that you are a child of God and an heir to His kingdom? **What can you do to remind yourself who you are in Christ even when you are facing rough circumstances?**

Daily Challenge:

#princess

☐ Jesus is the Son of God. Because of Him, you are the daughter of the King...you are a princess. Today, hit your knees and pray to your Father in Heaven the prayer that Jesus taught us to pray, the Lord's Prayer. (See Appendix 4)

☐ Share a video, image, or your written testimony with other sisters in Christ in the "Because He Said So" Facebook group. Please use the hashtags #princess and #iambecausehesaidso on all social media posts.

Visit Facebook.com/groups/iambecausehesaidso to join the community!

Day 17

I am... WEALTHY

"So, you are no longer a slave, but God's child; and since you are his child, God has made you also an heir."

Galatians 4:7

I love a good talk show. A few years ago, I saw one that featured a brother and sister who grew up in poverty. They lived with their mom in the same small house where she had been raised. Their mom worked several jobs and struggled month after month to put food on the table and pay the bills. When their mom passed away, they went back to that house where they grew up so that they could get her belongings. They went up to the attic and began going through the boxes that had been there since before their mom had been born. There they found a crumpled up brown bag. Most people would have thrown the bag out with the trash, but the brother took a peek inside and saw seven baseball cards that had belonged to his great grandfather. Thinking that the cards might have some value, they put them to the side and finished their task at hand. When they finally got to an appraiser, they realized that the cards were in pristine condition and worth millions! WOW! Their entire childhood they had lived in poverty, yet, the entire time they had been rich! All they had to do was go up and seek what had been left to them by their great-grandfather.

This story is an illustration of how most people tend to live their daily lives. Chances are that you live like you are poor, when you are indeed rich. You allow the circumstances of life to make you feel worthless and hopeless—when in fact, Romans 8:17 gives you an assurance that you are co-heirs with Christ. Because of God's work through Jesus, you have the riches of His son in an everlasting hope. The inheritance of Christ is yours! Now, let me be clear, I am not pretending for a second that money isn't important in this world. You need money to survive. However, I believe that God wants you to not only survive but thrive.

> No matter the monetary situation you may live with on this earth, *one day* you will walk on streets of gold and live in mansions of glory with our Heavenly Father.

How do you thrive when you may be struggling to pay the bills? You trust in Him and His provision. You claim the riches of His love, grace and mercy. As Lauren Daigle says in her song, "Everything": "Even the sparrow has a place to lay its head, so why would I let worries steal my breath? Even the roses, You have glowed them brilliant red; still I'm the one You love more than this. You give me everything, everything I need."

Jesus' words in Matthew 6:33 direct you to live life seeking Him first, believing that He will provide everything you need and more. He also reassures you in John 10:10 that He came to give you life, life abundant! So, today I ask you, Sister…which side of the comma are you living on? Are you just living life focused primarily on what you don't have, a life of scarcity? Or, are you claiming the riches of your inheritance as a daughter of Heaven and living the abundant life He came to give?

When I was a little girl, I thought any house with stairs was a mansion, and anyone who lived in a "stair-house" was rich. No matter the monetary situation you may live with on this earth, one day you will walk on streets of gold and live in mansions of glory with our Heavenly Father. "So that in the ages to come He might show the surpassing riches of His grace in kindness toward us in Christ Jesus" (Ephesians 2:7). The inheritance of Christ is yours! Claim it now and learn to live a life rich in Him!

So today and every day moving forward, when you find yourself measuring your net worth by your bank account or the profit of your IRA, cash in your value as a treasured child of God and exclaim, "**I am wealthy...because He said so!**"

Prayer

Dear Lord, Please forgive me when I stress out about what I don't have—whether it be relationships, abilities, or finances. Instead, I want to praise You for what I do have - I am wealthy beyond measure in You. Help me to claim the riches of my inheritance and choose to live an abundant life today and every day. In Jesus' name and for the Father's glory, Amen.

READ MORE
God's Word says you are wealthy...

Psalm 1:1-3 • Isaiah 61:7 • Matthew 6:19-21

Luke 15:31 • Romans 11:33 • 1 Timothy 6:17-19

Have you ever before thought about all of the riches that you have in Christ? **When you think of being rich or wealthy, what comes to mind immediately? Reread the devotional and answer the same question.**

Daily Challenge:

#wealthy

◯ Believing that you are rich in Him, stretch yourself and generously give beyond what you might ordinarily do for someone. (Examples: give a bigger tip, make a donation, or pay for someone's meal the next time you are out to eat)

◯ Share a video, image, or your written testimony with other sisters in Christ in the "Because He Said So" Facebook group. Please use the hashtags #wealthy and #iambecausehesaidso on all social media posts.

Visit Facebook.com/groups/iambecausehesaidso to join the community!

Day 18

I am...
BEAUTIFUL

"You are altogether beautiful; there is no flaw in you."

Song of Songs 4:7

If I think really hard, I can remember a time as a small girl, when I felt beautiful. Not nearly as difficult to recall are the feelings I experienced when I looked at myself right after entering puberty. Gazing in the mirror at my reflection, I saw a girl who had developed new curves and who had added a few pounds to the scale. I saw a girl who had an oily sheen to her face accented by red bumps known as pimples or zits. And thanks to a lengthy visit with Dr. McKinley, the local orthodontist, I saw a metal mouth glistening from the mirror! UGH! I remember speaking out loud to that young girl in the mirror…"You are ugly!" These feelings only seemed to magnify over the years through the highs and lows of surging hormones, not to mention the fact that I compared myself to all the other girls my age featured in Seventeen Magazine. If only my Calvin Klein jeans looked as good on me as they did on

Brooke Shields. If only my Stridex acne pads could really wipe away MY pimples. If only.

I wish I could tell you that as my teenage years gave way to my twenties and thirties that I became less hard on myself, but I can't. As a matter of fact, it seems as if society's demands to look good become more and more demanding. And now, as a middle-aged woman, I find myself still struggling—only now, instead of counting zits, I'm counting wrinkles.

Are you like me, Sister? Are you still looking in that full-length mirror and speaking to yourself in ways that you would never speak to another woman? Are you still thinking that you don't measure up because of a number on the scale or imperfections on your face? If so, remember that you are God's masterpiece and stop it! Stop the self-scrutiny. Turn your eyes from the mirror and focus them toward heaven. Your beauty is not determined by the standards of this world but by who you are in Christ. God loves you for who you are on the inside! Despite your appearance, despite how you feel about yourself, you were made new in Christ. The words of 2 Corinthians 4:16-17 assure you, "Therefore we do not lose heart. Though outwardly we are wasting away, yet inwardly we are being renewed day by day…. So, you must fix your eyes not on what is seen, but on what is unseen."

> Turn your eyes from the mirror and focus them toward Heaven. Your beauty is not determined by the standards of this world but by *who you are in Christ*.

So today and every day moving forward, when you don't feel beautiful, I encourage you to get up, wash your face, brush your teeth, and look confidently into that mirror. Ignore the actual image that is staring at you and look deeper. Knowing that God sees you through the lens of Christ smile and say, "**I am beautiful…because He said so!**"

Prayer

Dear Lord, When all I can see are my imperfections, open my eyes to see myself the way that You do - through the lens of Christ and His sacrifice on the cross. Thank You for making me beautiful through His blood and renewing me day after day. Let my self-image be based on the inner beauty that You see because of Jesus in my life. In Jesus' name and for the Father's glory, Amen.

READ MORE

God's Word says you are beautiful...

Psalm 45:11 • 1 Samuel 16:7 • Song of Songs 2:2

Song of Songs 2:10 • Ecclesiastes 3:11

Are there parts of your life that you are afraid He can't transform into something beautiful? **If so, list them and turn them over to Him in prayer. What beautiful things do you recognize in yourself?**

Daily Challenge:

#beautiful

☐ Be bold! Take a selfie when you wake up, before you are all made-up and dressed for your day. Post the image on social media with the words, "I am beautiful, because He said so!"

☐ Share a video, image, or your written testimony with other sisters in Christ in the "Because He Said So" Facebook group. Please use the hashtags #beautiful and #iambecausehesaidso on all social media posts.

Visit Facebook.com/groups/iambecausehesaidso to join the community!

Day 19

I am...
CHERISHED

"She is worth far more than rubies."

Proverbs 31:10

It was a cold winter's night in December while sipping champagne in front of the fireplace that I spotted it. Something was in the bottom of my fluted crystal glass! When I looked up to tell my boyfriend, Chris, about the foreign object in my bubbly, he was on one knee. He popped the question, and within a very few minutes, I had an engagement ring on my finger and a wedding date on the calendar! I was getting married!

Over the next few months, everywhere I went, people grabbed my left hand to check out the bling and shared kind words about how pretty my new ring was. However, I'll never forget one of my friends who lived far away, asking me about where my ring was ranked in the three C's: Cut, Carats, and Clarity. Honestly, I was taken aback and a little offended; what did it even matter?

But I explained that the ring was a marquee shaped diamond that measured almost a carat. As far as the third C...Clarity, I didn't know how it rated, nor did I care. You see, Chris was a struggling graduate student pursuing his doctorate, and to say that he made sacrifices to purchase that ring for me would be an understatement. If my new diamond had flaws, I didn't see them. When I looked at the ring, I saw it sparkling as a beautiful expression of my future husband's love and sacrifice. I cherished it.

When you cherish something, you hold it dear. You protect it and care for it lovingly because of its value to you. The rating systems of the world would have you believe that you are worthless due to your specks of sin and shortcomings. It would have you believe that there is no treasure inside you. But there is another C that isn't part of any jeweler's assessment. The C that I am talking about is Christ. And, because of Christ's sacrifice, God sees you as flawless—even precious! "Since you are precious in My sight, since you are honored and I love you..." (Isaiah 43:4a).

> You don't have to pretend to be perfect; Christ has *made you perfect.* Even more, He has set you *free!*

No fake treasure here; no cubic zirconia! You don't have to pretend to be perfect; Christ has made you perfect. Even more, He has set you free! Because of Him, you are free to be "real"—just who He created you to be. Your blemishes are not seen because of the brilliance of Jesus. Instead of rating you based on the number of specks in your soul, your God finds your value by searching your heart. "Blessed are the pure in heart, for they shall see God" (Matthew 5:8). Jesus came to earth to remove the stain of sin and, because of Him, you have value. You are indeed worth more than rubies.

In Psalm 17:8 David says, "Keep me as the apple of your eye; hide me in the shadow of your wings." This is David's way of proclaiming that he is cherished, kept safe, protected, and valued. My sweet sister, you are cherished by your Heavenly Father! Christ paid a ransom for your soul. God sent His son to pay for your sins because you are His treasured child.

So today and every day moving forward, when you find yourself focusing on your flaws, remember David's words, and declare, "**I am cherished...because He said so!**"

Prayer

Dear Lord, I don't have the words to say how much it means that You cherish me. You take care of me by surrounding me with Your love and blessings. You value me as if I were a precious gem, perfect in every way, because of Jesus' sacrifice. I don't deserve this, Lord, but I thank You for making me worth cherishing through Christ. In Jesus' name and for the Father's glory, Amen.

READ MORE

God's Word says you are cherished...

Deuteronomy 32:10-11 • Psalm 17:8

Psalm 23 • Zechariah 2:8

Do you believe that God proved His love for you by sacrificing His Son for your sins? **How does God remind you that you are the apple of His eye and cherished by Him in every way?**

Daily Challenge:

#cherished

☐ Today as you notice the different jewels being worn by those around you, send up a prayer to your Heavenly Father and thank Him for cherishing you more than any precious gemstone.

☐ Share a video, image, or your written testimony with other sisters in Christ in the "Because He Said So" Facebook group. Please use the hashtags #cherished and #iambecausehesaidso on all social media posts.

Visit Facebook.com/groups/iambecausehesaidso to join the community!

Day 20

I am...
BELOVED

"For I am convinced that neither death, nor life, nor angels, nor principalities, nor things present, nor things to come, nor powers, nor height, nor depth, nor any other created thing, will be able to separate us from the love of God, which is in Christ Jesus our Lord."

Romans 8:38-39

I don't have any tattoos, but I am fascinated by them. I can't imagine that I would ever get a tattoo myself, because I am such a baby when it comes to pain and needles. However, this tattoo craze that is such a part of our culture now is very interesting to me. When I was growing up, tattoos were for bikers, sailors, and thugs. Now it seems as everyone has a tattoo; their popularity has skyrocketed. Studies show that 40% of millennials have at least one tattoo. These perpetual body decorations come in all shapes and sizes. Most tattoos have deep meaning to the person and serve as a permanent reminder of a special person or event. These pieces of body art show the great love and passion for that someone or something the tattooed person holds dear. Without a doubt, you have to really love someone to have their name tattooed on your bicep...forever!

There is a distinct difference between loving someone/something and considering them/it "beloved." The key difference is that beloved denotes a deep relationship. Beloved signifies that someone is held dear and close to the heart, an intimate connection. One might first think of falling in love in the romantic and passionate sense, but in actuality a friend, spouse, child, mother, father, uncle, aunt, etc., with whom one shares a deep affection can be referred to as a beloved.

Rejoice, my sister, and search no more! You are beloved by your Father!

Women, especially, long to be loved and cherished. We crave deep, heartfelt relationships. We yearn to be beloved. Many of us spend a great deal of our lives searching for someone, anyone, to give us that type of adoration. Rejoice, my sister, and search no more! You are beloved by your Father! I encourage you to mediate on the words from our spotlight scripture again and hear the passion in the passage: "For I am convinced that neither death, nor life, nor angels, nor principalities, nor things present, nor things to come, nor powers, nor height, nor depth, nor any other created thing, will be able to separate us from the love of God, which is in Christ Jesus our Lord" (Romans 8:38-39). These verses are scripted with powerful words that paint the beautiful picture of how deeply your God cares for you.

Never allow yourself to doubt it; you are beloved by your Heavenly Father. Jesus bore the marks of God's love for you on His hands and feet—not tattoos, but scars from his sacrifice. "Behold, I have inscribed you on the palms of My hands" (Isaiah 49:16). Oh, may the name of Jesus be forever engraved on your heart!

So today and every day moving forward, when you wonder if you are loved, bring your hands to your heart, take a deep breath, and speak softly the words that will remind you of His great and fervent love for you, "**I am beloved...because He said so!**"

Prayer

Dear Lord, Just as Your love for me was written on Your hands and feet, I want Your name to be forever imprinted on my heart. Thank You for calling me Your "beloved" and for pouring out Your life and love for me. I will never be alone because I know that I am Yours and that You truly love me. In Jesus' name and for the Father's glory, Amen.

READ MORE

God's Word says you are beloved...

Isaiah 30:18 • Song of Songs 6:3 • Jeremiah 24:7

Romans 8:38-39 • 1 Peter 5:7

Is there any way to fully describe God's love for you? **How would you describe what it feels like to be God's "beloved"? How can you share that love with others?**

Daily Challenge:

◯ Set an alarm on your phone today for 8:38 and label the alarm, "I am beloved". From 8:38 until 8:39 read and reread Romans 8:38-39

◯ Share a video, image, or your written testimony with other sisters in Christ in the "Because He Said So" Facebook group. Please use the hashtags #beloved and #iambecausehesaidso on all social media posts.

Visit Facebook.com/groups/iambecausehesaidso to join the community!

Day 21

I am...
BLESSED

"Blessed is she who believed that He would fulfill His promises to her."

Luke 1:45

I distinctly remember the first time I realized that I was blessed. I was about six years old standing in my aunt's kitchen when I saw a "feed the world" type of commercial. It showed malnourished children from third world countries. The children were filmed unclothed and standing in the worst possible conditions. My heart broke, and I cried tears of sadness for them. I realized at that moment God had blessed me with a different set of circumstances than those children, and I wanted to help. In response to the commercial's call to action, a plea for us to send in money for the cause, I told my mom that I wanted to help them. It was a great feeling to know that I was able to provide something to ease their desperate need, even if it was only a few dollars.

You're probably just like me; when you think of being blessed, you think of the blessings of strong relationships with family and friends, vibrant health, and financial security. These are all indeed gifts from God of which you are to be thankful. But the New Testament references some form of being blessed more than 120 times, none of which have anything to do with these blessings of the flesh. God's Word defines blessed as "made holy." To be made holy is to be set apart by God for a special use or purpose. Oh, how I desire for God to use me for His purpose!

A look at Jesus' teaching on the Beatitudes illustrates that it is not your perfect life conditions or monetary prosperity that labels you as blessed. Jesus is stating, in a most poetic way, that when you depend on Him in all life's circumstances and seek Him first, you will be blessed, made holy to be used by Him for a purpose. In Genesis 12:2 God tells Abraham that He is going to bless him so that he can be a blessing. Sister, you are like Abraham. You are blessed, made holy in Christ, so that you can bless others! You want to be like that person in the spotlight scripture who is

Blessed are the *poor in spirit*, for theirs is the kingdom of heaven.

Blessed are they *who mourn*, for they will be comforted.

Blessed are the *meek*, for they will inherit the land.

Blessed are they who *hunger and thirst for righteousness*, for they will be satisfied.

Blessed are the *merciful*, for they will be shown mercy.

Blessed are the *clean of heart*, for they will see God.

Blessed are the *peacemakers*, for they will be called children of God.

Blessed are they who are *persecuted for the sake of righteousness*, for theirs is the kingdom of heaven.

Matthew 5:3-10

planted by the water yielding fruit. "But the fruit of the Spirit is love, joy, peace, forbearance, kindness, goodness, faithfulness, gentleness and self-control" (Galatians 5:22-23). Your spiritual fruits are the tools that you use to bless others!

Whatever your current state of affairs, if you are delighting in your Heavenly Father, meditating on Him day and night, and trusting Him to care for your every need, you are indeed blessed. Your blessings should urge you to answer His call to action and be a blessing to all mankind.

So today and every day moving forward, when you feel down, count your many blessings. Name them one by one, get on your knees, and with overflowing gratitude repeat the words, **"I am blessed, because He said so!"**

Prayer

Dear Lord, I am so grateful for every blessing, both big and small, in my life. Thank You for the people, provision, and peace that You provide me. Thank You for my greatest blessing - Jesus. Because of Him, my blessings are eternal. Lord, help me find ways to use my blessings to bless others and point them to You. In Jesus' name and for the Father's glory, Amen.

READ MORE

God's Word says you are blessed...

Numbers 6:24-26 • Deuteronomy 28:15

2 Corinthians 9:8 • Ephesians 1:3 • James 1:17

Have you ever actually counted your blessings one by one? **Even if you've done this before, make a list of your blessings. Which blessings do you feel God gave you specifically so that you could be a blessing to others? Who can you bless today?**

Daily Challenge:

#blessed

- ☐ Download the song "The Blessing" by Kari Jobe and Cody Carnes. As you listen, remember that you are creating eternal blessings, for generations to come, by following Jesus.

- ☐ Share a video, image, or your written testimony with other sisters in Christ in the "Because He Said So" Facebook group. Please use the hashtags #blessed and #iambecausehesaidso on all social media posts.

Visit Facebook.com/groups/iambecausehesaidso to join the community!

Day 22

I am...
JOYFUL

"When anxiety was great within me, your consolation brought joy to my soul!"

Psalm 94:19

"Happy" by Pharrell, "Don't Worry Be Happy" by Bobby McFerrin, and an oldie, but goodie, that I sang at the top of my lungs as a preschooler, "Happiest Girl in the Whole USA" by Donna Fargo, (if you've not heard it, it's worth Googling) are just a few of the songs in the Top 20 "Happy" Songs of all time. There is a huge movement in pop culture today to be happy. It's not surprising when you think about what a typical day in our life looks like. We get up, get dressed, and get to work. Run by the grocery, come home and prepare supper. Throw the dishes in the sink and head out the door for a meeting. Come home, put the kids to bed, pay some bills, and fold a load of laundry! STOP THE INSANITY! It is hard to be happy in the hustle or in the humdrum of life.

I'm going to be blunt...Sister, you and I are missing the mark. We need to stop searching for happiness and instead begin seeking JOY. In other words, we need to choose to be joyful in every situation we face. Happiness is an emotion, a mood, that is dependent on external circumstances, while joy is a continual feeling of gladness, peace, and serenity that is totally independent of your circumstances. There's a BIG difference. Joy! THAT'S what you need to get through the ups and downs of life.

> Happiness is an emotion, a mood, that is dependent on *external circumstances*, while joy is a continual feeling of gladness, peace, and serenity that is totally *independent* of your circumstances.

In Paul's letter to the Philippians, also known as the Letter of Joy, he encourages you to be joyful in all situations. Isn't it ironic that he wrote this letter from a cell in a Roman prison? "Rejoice in the Lord always. Again, I will say, rejoice! Let your gentleness be known to all men. The Lord is at hand. Be anxious for nothing, but in everything by prayer and supplication, with thanksgiving, let your requests be made known to God; and the peace of God, which surpasses all understanding, will guard your hearts and minds through Christ Jesus" (Philippians 4:4-7). What an example this is for you that joy is not found in the things and circumstances of your life.

The question then becomes, how do you find joy? And the answer, my friend, is easy; the way to find joy is to find Jesus. He is the source of your joy. Christ in you means that joy is in you. It's already there! You just have to find it and cultivate it until it grows and matures. You have to choose to live joyfully by focusing on and trusting in your Lord rather than the conditions of your life. You must seek Him first through spending time with Him in His word and prayer, and when you do...it is certain that you will find joy.

Multiple times throughout His Word He tells you to rejoice! Jesus came to give life, life abundant. So, you should live in the ecstasy and elation of this gift of life that He sacrificed Himself to give. Stay in The Word, communicate with Him in prayer, and ask Him to grow your joy in Him every day. "These things have I spoken unto you, that my joy might remain in you, and that your joy might be full" (John 15:11). God wants you to live a life of joy in Him!

My stressed-out sister… stop worrying about being happy! You simply need to make the decision to choose joy. Don't become so overwhelmed with the chaos of your life that you forget to passionately pursue Him in the moments of madness. Take a breath in the middle of bedlam and look to your Savior and smile when you are surrounded by stress.

So today and every day moving forward, when sadness seems to feel your soul, find the joy that already abides in you. Because of His Spirit in you, you can always delight in Him. So, jubilantly proclaim, **"I am joyful…because He said so!"**

Prayer

Dear Lord, Forgive me for the times that I feel stressed and depressed by circumstances. Teach me how to choose joy in the midst of desperation. Help me cultivate and grow the joy of Christ that is inside me so that it overflows and touches everyone I am with. May my joy in You be what attracts others to know You more. In Jesus' name and for the Father's glory, Amen.

READ MORE

God's Word says you are joyful...

Psalm 16:11 • Psalm 30:5

Isaiah 12:6 • John 15:9-11 • Romans 12:12

Before reading this devotional, did you know that there was a difference between happiness and joy? **Now that you know, what can you do to grow the incredible joy of Christ that is deep within you?**

Daily Challenge:

☐ Write Psalm 118:24 on your hand. When people ask you about it, put a smile on your face and tell them joyfully, "Today is the day the Lord has made; rejoice and be glad in it."

☐ Share a video, image, or your written testimony with other sisters in Christ in the "Because He Said So" Facebook group. Please use the hashtags #joyful and #iambecausehesaidso on all social media posts.

Visit Facebook.com/groups/iambecausehesaidso to join the community!

Day 23

I am...
PEACEFUL

"You will keep in perfect peace those whose minds are steadfast, because they trust in you."

Isaiah 26:3

Have you ever heard the saying, "Calgon, take me away!"? It comes from a television commercial launched in the 1970s for Calgon, a bubble bath product. This ad features a woman wearing a fluffy pink robe dealing with several chaotic scenarios. As the tension rises, she lifts her hands in the air and says, "Calgon, take me away!" The next scene shows her in a bath full of bubbles, relaxing. I must admit that this commercial resonates with me deeply. Anyone that knows me will attest that there is nothing I love more at the end of a stressful day than a long, hot bubble bath.

Yesterday joy was our focus; today, we explore peace. These two concepts really go hand in hand. It is indeed hard to find either when you consider all the stresses that come from the frenzied life you lead. Is it any wonder that more than 65% of American women are on anxiety medication? From the moment your feet hit the floor, you are being pulled in every direction. You have home and family responsibilities, work duties, and community obligations that often leave you without a moment to even catch your breath. The anxiety that you may feel from the chaos, stress, and worry that comes from this demanding life can sometimes seem too much. It can cause you to throw your hands in the air and long for your own "Calgon take me away" moment.

> By accepting the gift of salvation, you are filled with the Holy Spirit; and thus, *peace abides in you.*

In the book of Daniel, you see someone who remains peaceful despite an incredibly stressful situation. Daniel worked for King Darius. The king, tricked by some of his advisors, sent out a decree forbidding his people from praying to anyone but the king for 30 days. Did that cause Daniel anxiety? No! He calmly went home and continued his prayer life, praying daily to his Heavenly Father and focusing on his God. And, as the story goes, he was thrown into the lion's den for breaking the law. The king finds him the day after his punishment, sitting as cool as a cucumber, proclaiming how great his God is for shutting the mouths of the lions and keeping him safe. If only you could find this kind of peace in your own personal "lion's den"!

The truth is that you can! Like joy, true peace is found in Christ. If you've got Jesus, you've got peace! In John 14:27 Jesus said, "Peace I leave with you; my peace I give to you." By accepting the gift of salvation, you are filled with the Holy Spirit; and thus, peace abides in you. Focusing on your God and literally surrendering your situations and your circumstances to His will, you will experience His peace. You can, like Daniel, remain peaceful in the pandemonium.

So today and every day moving forward, when you are feeling the weight of this world around you and you sense a panic attack coming on, close your eyes, take in a deep breath, and surrender the situation to your Heavenly Father. Then whisper the words, "**I am peaceful...because He said so!**"

Prayer

Dear Lord, Thank You for giving me Your peace in the pandemonium of my daily life. I know that with You, I can experience calm no matter my circumstances. When I start to fret with frustrations that I can't control, remind me that it's Your Holy Spirit inside me that silences the stresses of the world. Use me, Lord, to show others that there is serenity in the Savior. In Jesus' name and for the Father's glory, Amen.

READ MORE

God's Word says you are peaceful...

Psalm 29:11 • Psalm 119:165 • John 14:27

Philippians 4:7 • Colossians 1:19-20 • 2 Thessalonians 3:16

When life is chaotic, do you remember that the God of peace is deep inside you? **What actions could you do to bring His peace in your life? How can you share His peace with others?**

Daily Challenge:

#peaceful

☐ Take a walk today. Listen to worship music and find peace in Him. Be sure to marvel at His creations during your quiet time. Pray for someone else who needs to experience His peace.

☐ Share a video, image, or your written testimony with other sisters in Christ in the "Because He Said So" Facebook group. Please use the hashtags #peaceful and #iambecausehesaidso on all social media posts.

Visit Facebook.com/groups/iambecausehesaidso to join the community!

Day 24

I am...
ENOUGH

"Whom have I in heaven but you? And earth has nothing I desire besides you. My flesh and my heart may fail, but God is the strength of my heart and my portion forever."

Psalm 73:25-26

Being a petite kid, I always felt like I didn't measure up…literally. I cannot count the number of times I stood back to back with someone in a height challenge and came up short. And there was teasing! Other kids called me inappropriate things like "midget" and "dwarf". And to add to my feelings that being short was a "shortcoming", out came a popular song entitled, "Short People". The lyrics of this tune added to my feelings of inadequacy through the words of the main verse - "I don't want no short people 'round here". One might say that I had a bit of a complex about my height, or lack thereof. I definitely believed that I was too short to measure up. The good news is that as I grew into a young woman I began to worry less and less about my height. The bad news is that the measuring had only just begun.

Whether you are keeping up with the Joneses or the Kardashians, you live in a world full of measuring sticks. Chances are you are continually comparing yourself to others and assessing who has the best, most, newest, biggest, shiniest, etc. Society has programmed you to think that you should be superwomen. You are expected to be June Cleaver, (Super mom and homemaker from the 50s TV show, "Leave it to Beaver"), Sheryl Sandberg (COO of Facebook), and Mother Teresa (Saint) all rolled into one. The result is that all of these expectations and comparisons leave you feeling like you are not enough. And the truth is…you aren't! No matter how many positive podcasts you listen to or motivational memes you read that try to convince you otherwise, you simply aren't enough on your own.

> God promises to *never forsake us* in our time of weakness; so, rest assured that God sent Jesus to save us. He is the *Savior.*

It is time for you to put down your ruler and pick up His word. It is in the truth of these pages you find that you can never perform your way to being enough. There will always be people who can accomplish more than you. And that's okay…God doesn't gauge your worth based on your performance or how your execution of tasks rates in contrast to others. You weren't created for the purpose of racking up accomplishments. You were created for the purpose of having a relationship with Him. Because Christ is in you, you aren't judged by how you measure up in this world, but by what is in your heart. "But the Lord said to Samuel, "Do not look on his appearance or on the height of his stature, because I have rejected him. For the Lord sees not as man sees: man looks on the outward appearance, but the Lord looks on the heart" (1 Samuel 16:7).

Sister, the fact is that you will never measure up in all of the different roles you play in this world. That's okay; embrace it! God's word assures you two things with certainty: 1. By yourself you are not enough. 2. In Him, you are more than enough. He is all that you need!

So today and every day moving forward, when the lies of the world seep in telling you that you're inadequate, remember His promises to you in His word and claim, "**I am enough…because He said so!**"

Prayer

Dear Lord, Thank You that I don't have to worry anymore about measuring up to the standards of this world. Because of Christ I have no more concerns about being adequate or capable enough. You have made me "more than enough" in Him! With Christ I can confidently handle anything that comes at me. In Jesus' name and for the Father's glory, Amen.

READ MORE

God's Word says you are enough...

Psalm 16:5 • Psalm 46:5 • Psalm 73:25-26

1 Corinthians 1:30-31 • Philippians 4:13

Are you sometimes worried about how you compare with others? **In what ways do you find yourself comparing your life, circumstances, possessions, looks, etc to others and how can you give those to God?**

Daily Challenge:

#enough

- ☐ Text the "praise hands" emoji to someone who struggles with feeling like they don't measure up. When they question what the text means, respond, "Just praising God that we are enough in Him!"

- ☐ Share a video, image, or your written testimony with other sisters in Christ in the "Because He Said So" Facebook group. Please use the hashtags #enough and #iambecausehesaidso on all social media posts.

Visit Facebook.com/groups/iambecausehesaidso to join the community!

Day 25

I am...

UNDERSTOOD

"You know when I sit down and when I rise up; you discern my thoughts from afar."

Psalm 139:2

My oldest son, Michael, is an electrical engineer who lived at home while earning his college degree. The things that boy was learning! There was no way I would ever be able to help him proof his work or study for a test. It wasn't just the 3-page long equations one might expect with this complex field of study; I didn't recognize any of it! The vocabulary was completely unfamiliar—Snubber, Bipolar Junction Transistor, Diodes! And the acronyms! No way! ASIC, IBO, LNA, and P-P, just to name a few. These concepts are literally a foreign language to me, LOL. (FYI: LOL is actually an acronym in electrical engineering, and it doesn't stand for "laugh out loud"!) Obviously, Michael and I were not going to connect through what he was learning. Thankfully, we have many other areas in our lives that we do connect and understand each other.

Have you ever thought that no one understands you—no one really "gets you"? Everyone wants to be understood. How wonderful it is to know that your Creator knows you and understands you. Jeremiah 1:5 reminds you that since you were formed in your mother's womb, He has known you. If you have trouble comprehending this, look to Jesus. He walked on this earth to bear the burdens of your journey. He knew temptation, frustration, rejection, sorrow, ridicule, and loneliness. "For we do not have a high priest who is unable to empathize with our weaknesses, but we have one who has been tempted in every way, just as we are—yet he did not sin." (Hebrews 4:15).

> Our Heavenly Father even *understands you* when you don't know how to articulate your *own* thoughts.

Our Heavenly Father even understands you when you don't know how to articulate your own thoughts. "In the same way, the Spirit helps us in our weakness. We do not know what we ought to pray for, but the Spirit himself intercedes for us through wordless groans. And he who searches our hearts knows the mind of the Spirit, because the Spirit intercedes for God's people in accordance with the will of God" (Romans 8:26-27). Isn't that astounding? He translates your thoughts!

Not only do you want to be understood, you also want to understand. You have a desire to understand the how's and why's of your worldly circumstances. And as much as you want to know the answers to all of life's questions, you might never be able to identify the reasons for the things you experience on earth until you are with Him in eternity. "Jesus replied, 'You don't understand what I am doing now, but some day you will'" (John 13:7). Sister, that is where faith comes in. Proverbs 3:5 reminds you, "Trust in the Lord with all your heart and lean not on your own understanding." You have to trust in the fact that because He knows you and understands you that He will always do what is best for you in His will.

What a relief! God knows your hidden hurts, your shameful sins, and the deepest desires of your heart; you can trust Him with everything. There is nothing about you that He doesn't know and understand. And guess what? Because of the cross, He loves you and welcomes you into His arms no matter what kind of crazy you have going on inside!

So today and every day moving forward, when you feel like you don't understand your circumstances or that no one understands you, remind yourself that the Creator of the Universe "gets you" and that's enough. Rest in His promises and proclaim out loud, "**I am understood…because He said so!**"

Prayer

Dear Lord, I am so grateful that You have walked where I am walking and that You have felt the emotions that I am feeling. Thank You for being the God who understands me – even when I don't understand myself. Thank You for the gift of Your Holy Spirit that intercedes for me when I don't know what to say. In Jesus' name and for the Father's glory, Amen.

READ MORE

God's Word says you are understood...

1 Chronicles 28:9 • Psalm 139:2-5

John 11:35 • Hebrews 4:13-16

Do you ever feel like no one really understands where you are coming from or what you are feeling? **God understands! How does knowing this affect your attitude toward others and toward yourself reflecting that belief?**

Daily Challenge:

#understood

- ☐ Have a conversation today with someone who has different views than you. Try to understand their perspective. Listen to bond not to respond. Let them see Jesus in you. Pray the Prayer of St. Assisi before you talk with them. (See Appendix 5)

- ☐ Share a video, image, or your written testimony with other sisters in Christ in the "Because He Said So" Facebook group. Please use the hashtags #understood and #iambecausehesaidso on all social media posts.

Visit Facebook.com/groups/iambecausehesaidso to join the community!

Day 26

I am...
PROTECTED

"The LORD will keep you from all harm--he will watch over your life."

Psalm 121:7

Have you been through an airport lately? There are so many precautions in place to keep us safe. You have to show your ID and your boarding pass, take off your shoes, take out all electronics, pass all of your bags through an x-ray machine and walk through a metal detector or a full-body scanner. If that's not enough, in some cases, like a recent time when I went through security, you even have to be patted down. It's not fun! Even though the professionals explain each step of the process as they inspect your body to ensure you aren't a threat it feels so invasive. As yucky as it is, everyone endures this process because you want your flight to be as safe as possible.

Everyone wants to be kept safe—safe from harm, safe from

sickness, safe from financial loss, etc. As a matter of fact, people spend a lot of money on protecting themselves and the ones they love. Helmets, masks, sunglasses, sunscreen, hand sanitizer, immunizations, security systems, passwords and insurance are just a few of the things that have been created to protect. Although people must take practical steps to safeguard themselves and those they love, it is important for you to realize that your God is the true source of safety.

Wanting to be protected is nothing new. It is a basic human desire. You see this in our spotlight scripture today which is an excerpt from Psalm 121. I encourage you to read the entire Psalm. It is one of 15 Psalms known as "The Songs of Ascent" or "Pilgrim Songs." These songs were sung by the Israelites as they took their yearly pilgrimages to Jerusalem for the religious festivals, where they would worship God. The Israelites' journeys were quite different from yours today. There was no airport security to ensure their safety. They faced serious dangers. Their enemies would often hide in the hills waiting to attack; thus, the travelers would sing Psalm 121:1-2, "I lift up my eyes to the mountains — where does my help come from? My help comes from the Lord, the Maker of heaven and earth." Perhaps my favorite image of God in this reading comes from verse 4: "...indeed, he who watches over Israel will neither slumber nor sleep." What assurance that must have been for the Israelites when night fell, and their weary bodies needed sleep. What assurance that gives you today knowing that God never takes his eyes off of you!

> The Lord is your fortified tower where you can run to be safe. Sister, you are safe in Him who holds you *close*.

The journeys of the Israelites were long and difficult, and, they could be dangerous. They trusted that God would keep them safe until they reached their destination. That certainly is a lesson for you to learn today. This journey called "life" can be hard, but The Creator of the Universe is here to protect you. Moreover, in Christ you have the assurance that when you reach your journey's end, that you will spend eternity with Him.

When I was a small girl and woke up in the middle of the night scared and longing to be protected, I would run to my parents' bed to be comforted until I fell back to sleep. Proverbs 18:10 is a reminder that the Lord is your fortified tower where you can run to be safe. My precious sister, you are safe in Him who holds you close. Go ahead and take precautions to live safely in today's world, but never doubt that the true source of your security is your refuge in Christ.

So today and every day moving forward, when you feel vulnerable and scared, "look up to the mountains," call out to the Almighty, your Shelter and Guard, and declare confidently, "**I am protected…because He said so!**"

Prayer

Dear Lord, Thank You for being the fortified tower that I can run to when I am afraid. Whenever I feel vulnerable— whether physically, emotionally or even spiritually, I promise to turn to You. You are my protector. Lord, when someone I know is scared or in need, help me share with them that security is found in the Savior. In Jesus' name and for the Father's glory, Amen.

READ MORE

God's Word says you are protected...

Psalm 121 • Psalm 139:5 • Proverbs 18:10

Isaiah 54:17 • 2 Thessalonians 3:3

Have you ever had to walk alone down a dark abandoned street at night? Did you feel afraid or unprotected? Did you call on God to be your source of security? **What areas of your life do you want God to protect?**

Daily Challenge:

#protected

- ☐ Today as you enter the passwords that protect your personal information, remind yourself that He keeps you safe. Thank God for covering you with His protection.

- ☐ Share a video, image, or your written testimony with other sisters in Christ in the "Because He Said So" Facebook group. Please use the hashtags #protected and #iambecausehesaidso on all social media posts.

Visit Facebook.com/groups/iambecausehesaidso to join the community!

Day 27

I am...
FEARLESS

"For God has not given us a spirit of fear, but of power and of love and of a sound mind."

2 Timothy 1:7

Perhaps you suffer from some of the most common phobias on the "Top 100 List of Phobias"—yes, there actually is a list! These fears range from the understandable, like fear of spiders, heights, and enclosed spaces, to the somewhat ludicrous, like the fear of buttons and couches. WHAT? Personally, I suffer from Ophidiophobia (fear of snakes) and Dentophobia (fear of the dentist). What about you...are you sometimes paralyzed by fear?

Fear is a natural and instinctive response to protect you, and it is much needed especially in our modern world. Today as you think about being fearless, I want to focus on a fear that you may not even be aware of. It's not the healthy fear that God created for your safety. It's a fear that lies so deep in your subconscious mind that it becomes the enemy's favorite weapon of deception because you don't even realize that it is paralyzing you. It is a multi-layered fear that keeps you stuck living a lukewarm life rather than one where you are passionately pursing your purpose in Him. If you dissect the layers of this fear, they would be:

1. The Fear of Rejection
2. The Fear of Failure
3. The Fear of Making a Mistake
4. The Fear of Change
5. The Fear of Being Judged
6. The Fear of Loneliness
7. The Fear of Inadequacy

Sister, I'm here to tell you that none of these fears are given to you by God to protect you from a life-threatening danger. These are fears, lies even, that prevent you from becoming all that you were created to be. Fear is a liar! Fear comes from the one who came to steal, kill and destroy. And there is only one remedy to combat this type of fear—and it is faith! You must choose faith over fear!

Our spotlight scripture today clearly states that God did not give you a spirit of timidity. As a matter of fact, in God's word, "Do not be afraid" is referenced in some form or fashion 365 times. That's a reminder for every day of the year to be fearless. Timidity doesn't come from the Lord. He doesn't move people for His purpose by making them timid. He moves people by causing them to make decisions based upon what is right regardless of the personal risks.

Today I challenge you to ask yourself a few questions: What has God called me to do? What is my purpose? What is holding me back from taking action toward that calling? What would I do if I truly believed that I could "do all things through Christ"? What would I do if I was truly fearless?

Next, decide to let all fear go, trust in Him, and take action. Faith is an action word! The Israelites had to step into the flowing water of the Jordan River before it parted. Likewise, you must take a step toward your passion and purpose, even if it is a small one, before He opens up the obstacles in your way.

So today and every day moving forward, when you feel scared to face the circumstances of your life, boldly claim His promises. Believe that He created you to be daring for Him. And with each step of your faith journey, look up, and bravely proclaim, **"I am fearless...because He said so!"**

Prayer

Dear Lord, Please forgive me when I allow my fears to hold me back from serving You. In a world that seems uncertain and even scary at times, remind me that I can put my trust in You. I am thankful that You didn't create me to live a life full of worry and anxiety. Thank You for creating me to walk with You, Father, in assurance and faith. In Jesus' name and for the Father's glory, Amen.

READ MORE

God's Word says you are fearless...

Psalm 16:8 • Psalm 46:1-3 • Proverbs 29:25

Isaiah 41:10-12 • Isaiah 12:2 • 1 Peter 5:7

Do you feel that at times you have been held back by fear? **List the fears that are holding you back. What can you do to become fearless for God?**

_____

_____

_____

Daily Challenge:

#fearless

☐ We all have fears. Pray today for a complete stranger about the fears that they may be facing. Ask God to help them choose faith over fear.

☐ Share a video, image, or your written testimony with other sisters in Christ in the "Because He Said So" Facebook group. Please use the hashtags #fearless and #iambecausehesaidso on all social media posts.

Visit Facebook.com/groups/iambecausehesaidso to join the community!

Day 28

I am... COURAGEOUS

> *"Be strong and courageous. Do not be afraid or terrified because of them, for the LORD your God goes with you; he will never leave you nor forsake you."*
>
> **Deuteronomy 31:6**

We know God loves us as a Father when He can reveal a deep spiritual lesson even from a simple children's story. Case in point: The Wizard of Oz. As Dorothy, Toto, The Scarecrow and The Tinman skipped down the famous yellow brick road toward The Land of Oz, they were startled by a lion. They should have been scared, really scared. Lions are, after all, the "King of the Beasts" due to the fact that they are the largest meat-eating animals in the world. But you know this story, right? This was no ordinary lion. This was a cowardly lion! And as much as he tried to put up a front to conceal his fears, he simply couldn't hide the truth— that he was terrified of everything. So, Dorothy befriended The Cowardly Lion and invited him to continue on the journey with her and her friends so that he could request courage from the esteemed wizard. Ultimately, the wizard gives the lion a medal for bravery. With tangible proof of his bravery, the lion realizes that he does have courage.

Yesterday you read that in Christ you are fearless. Fear is a state of mind that holds you back. But courage…courage is about taking action despite the fear. Courage moves you forward. And the only way to have courage is to make the decision to choose faith over fear!

> The only way to have courage is to make the decision to choose *faith over fear*!

In the Wizard of Oz story, you see a shift in the lion, who started out being cowardly, but became courageous. Why? Because the medal gave him faith. Like so many, you may put your faith in things or people, hoping that you will gain courage and confidence from them. This faith is misplaced. Faith that fosters courage comes only from God. For you to be fearless and move forward in courage, you must put all your faith in the One who died for you.

Queen Esther is a great example of choosing faith in God over her own fear. She was faced with the choice of risking it all to save her people or to allow fear to paralyze her, while her family and her people were slaughtered: "For if you remain silent at this time, relief and deliverance for the Jews will arise from another place, but you and your father's family will perish. And who knows but that you have come to your royal position for such a time as this?" (Esther 4:14). You see, a decree had been sent out to annihilate the Jews of the Kingdom. Secretly, being a Jew herself, Esther knew that she had to do something to intervene. She needed to talk with her husband, the king, but tradition dictated that the queen could not approach the king unless she was invited. Esther secretly sent a message to the Jewish people to let them know her plan: "Go, gather together all the Jews who are in Susa, and fast for me. Do not eat or drink for three days, night or day. I and my attendants will fast as you do. When this is done, I will go to the king, even though it is against the law. And if I perish, I perish" (Esther 4:16). She was willing to risk her life to save her people. After fasting and praying for three days, she overcame her fears and courageously stepped forward and approached King Xerxes. God gave her favor with the king and Queen Esther ultimately saved her people from obliteration. Her courage wasn't grounded in her belief in herself, her position as queen, or her natural abilities, but in the deliverance that could only come from her God!

Like you, Queen Esther was created on purpose for a purpose. By divine design, God has a mission for you to accomplish in this life. Often it takes courage to accomplish it, but you can't have courage without faith. Faith and courage are two sides of the same coin. Without faith, your subconscious mind jumps into protection mode and literally stops you from taking action. Sister, I don't know about you, but I want to have courage in my calling! I want that for you, too!

So today and every day moving forward, choose faith over fear. Bring out your inner Esther, face your personal mission and exclaim, **"I am courageous...because He said so!"**

Prayer

Dear Lord, Thank You for creating me on purpose for a purpose. Forgive me when I am afraid to take the needed steps toward that calling. Remind me, Lord, that choosing faith over fear shows total reliance on You. Complete surrender allows You to get all the credit. I pray that my life shows others to trust in You as they move forward in faith. In Jesus' name and for the Father's glory, Amen.

READ MORE

God's Word says you are courageous...

Joshua 1:9 • 1 Chronicles 28:20

Psalm 31:24 • 1 Corinthians 16:13

Is God calling you to do something that's outside your comfort zone—that requires courage? **What is it and how are you courageously taking action to accomplish His will?**

Daily Challenge:

#courageous

◯ Take action on your faith today. Share something on social media that lets people know that you are a believer and a proud child of God.

◯ Share a video, image, or your written testimony with other sisters in Christ in the "Because He Said So" Facebook group. Please use the hashtags #courageous and #iambecausehesaidso on all social media posts.

Visit Facebook.com/groups/iambecausehesaidso to join the community!

Day 29

I am...
STRONG

"But you, Lord, do not be far from me. You are my strength; come quickly to help me."

Psalm 22:19

The first time it happened, she was blindsided. She had gone to the grocery store and forgotten something that he told her to pick up. This aggravated him and made him so angry that he hit her. He slapped her across the face. And while this was the first time he struck her; it wasn't the last. By the time their first daughter was born, two years into the marriage, the physical and mental abuse had escalated. She knew she had to get out, but he had told her that he would never let her go. He had moved her thousands of miles away from her family. As the youngest of nine children, until this time in her life, she had always had someone to turn to for protection. Now, there was no one. She felt alone, helpless, and ashamed. It wasn't until Mark found himself another woman that he loosened the reins and let her go. After a five-year tumultuous marriage, she loaded her daughter and a few of their things in her little yellow Chevy Vega and made the freedom journey back to her hometown to start over. The struggle to raise a daughter as a single mother wasn't easy, but she did the best she could, sacrificing her needs for the welfare of her child.

At work she met a good man named Boyce, whom she and her daughter both adored. They were married, and he became the "daddy" her daughter had never had.

They built a beautiful life together, had another baby girl named Amanda, and filled their home with love and security. But this wouldn't last long. Only 12 years into the marriage, Boyce suddenly died. At the young age of 38,

> Let the weak say,
> *"I am strong."*

she became a widow and starting over as a single mom yet again. In less than 20 years this woman experienced being a high school student, an abused wife, a widow, and a single mother, twice.

Even though the above passage reads like the script of a Lifetime movie, it tells the story of the real-life drama of my mom, Lottie. To say that this five-foot, 95-pound woman is the strongest woman I know is an understatement, and she gives God all the glory for the strength that she found to endure all of these trying moments. What an example she has been to my sister, Amanda, and me! And, good news is that for the last 25 years, my mom has been blessed by God to be happily married to an incredible man known to all of us as Papa Jeff!

When you think of a strong woman, do you think first of the lady with well-defined muscles who attends cross-fit classes, or do you think of a woman, like my mother, who has been through the storms of life and survived, thrived even? I'm sure you have endured storms in your life, and very often, during those trying times, you don't feel strong. You may actually feel like you are simply going through the motions. Isaiah 40:29 reminds you that He gives power to the weary and strength to the weak. He promises to do in you what you can't do for yourself. The weaker you are, the more dependent you are on God. The more dependent you are on Him, the stronger you become. The challenges of life, the weights of the world, are like the plates slipped on a barbell. Although they are a heavy load to carry, they strengthen you because you must look to Him and have faith that

He is strong enough to lift the weight. When you believe that, you can rest in His strength. The apostle Paul explained why he would always boast in God's strength: "But he [God] said to me, 'My grace is sufficient for you, for my power is made perfect in your weakness.' Therefore, I will boast all the more gladly about my weaknesses, so that Christ's power may rest on me" (2 Corinthians 12:9).

In Joel 3:10, you are directed to recognize the strength of God by proclaiming, "Let the weak say, 'I am strong.'" Words have power. Philippians 4:13 promises that no matter what burdens are weighing you down, even though you are weak, you can do all things—handle all things—because Christ gives you strength!

So today and every day moving forward, when you are feeling feeble, exercise your strength muscles by hitting your knees in prayer...then stand up confidently and boastfully say in your weakness, **"I am strong...because He said so!"**

Prayer

Dear Lord, I come to You because, at times, I feel so weak and helpless. Remind me in these moments that Your power is made perfect in my weakness. Build up my spiritual, mental, emotional, and physical muscles to handle any situation I may face. Thank You for carrying me through this life with Your strength so that I can be strong in You. In Jesus' name and for the Father's glory, Amen.

READ MORE

God's Word says you are strong...

1 Chronicles 16:11 • Psalm 46:1-3 • Isaiah 30:15

Isaiah 40:29 • Nehemiah 8:10 • 2 Corinthians 12:10

Is your life making you feel drained, exhausted, overwhelmed, or weak? **If you gave God your weakness, and you started genuinely relying on His strength, how might your life be different?**

Daily Challenge:

#strong

☐ Push yourself today further than you think you can. Whether it's a mental or physical workout remind yourself that your strength comes from Him.

☐ Share a video, image, or your written testimony with other sisters in Christ in the "Because He Said So" Facebook group. Please use the hashtags #strong and #iambecausehesaidso on all social media posts.

Visit Facebook.com/groups/iambecausehesaidso to join the community!

Day 30

I am...

VICTORIOUS

"But thanks be to God! He gives us the victory through our Lord Jesus Christ."

1 Corinthians 15:57

Field Day! It's the day that elementary students anticipate all year. The day where students wear matching t-shirts, have no school lessons, and compete in all sorts of individual and team races and activities. However, for a girl who wasn't much of an athlete, Field Day always brought with it feelings of stress and inadequacy. The day for me was grueling. The words "50-Yard Dash", "Sack Race", and "3-Legged Race" make me feel anxious even to this day. Now don't get me wrong...I like to compete. I do, however, like to think that I have a chance to win! And when it came to these types of events as a small child, I didn't stand a chance. Then, one glorious year, the school added in some less physical competitions. When it was officially announced that there would be a math race and a spelling race added to that year's events, this runt of the class was thrilled. I actually felt like I had a shot at being a champion of a field day race. I believed in my ability to win! And that year, for the first time, and last time, in my school career, I came home from Field Day with a ribbon—1st Place in the Math Race and 3rd Place in the Spelling Race.

> Because of Jesus and His incredible sacrifice for you, *you win*, and you get the trophy of eternal life with Him!

Who would have ever bet on a victory from a team of underdogs named Shadrach, Meshack, and Abednego? Probably no one. These young men were arrested, tied up, and thrown into a blazing furnace after refusing to bow down to the golden idol of King Nebuchadnezzar. But they were victorious; they beat all the odds and survived the fire. And they didn't just survive. This trio came out of the blaze uncharred, praising their God and rejoicing!

Do you often experience the sweet smell of victory or does it seem like your life has been more about the agony of defeat? It is certainly easy to compare yourself to others and feel like you have a BIG "L" for "Loser" emblazoned on your forehead! Life can feel, at times, defeating. And oh, how the enemy wants you to throw in the towel and admit loss. But, my sister, there is cause to celebrate. You have ultimate victory in Jesus! "For everyone born of God overcomes the world. This is the victory that has overcome the world, even our faith" (1 John 5:4). Jesus overcame the grave and won the battle for you. When He rose from the dead, you became a victor, too. It doesn't matter whether you are the fastest and strongest or not. Because of Jesus and His incredible sacrifice for you, you win, and you get the trophy of eternal life with Him! And that's better than any championship you can earn on this earth.

So today and every day moving forward, when facing the battles that are ahead of you, believe that you will be triumphant. Stand on the platform of success and collect your award. You are a champion! And in giving your victory speech, proclaim your Lord and Savior as the source for all your winning feats and say, "**I am victorious...because He said so!**"

Prayer

Dear Lord, Forgive me when my visions are more focused on the victories of this world rather than the success of the Savior. Thank You that I am triumphant forever because of Jesus. No matter what the scoreboard of society says, I win with You. I praise You, Father, for my eternal victory in Christ! In Jesus' name and for the Father's glory, Amen.

READ MORE

God's Word says you are victorious...

Deuteronomy 20:4 • Joshua 10:8 • Proverbs 21:31

Romans 8:37 • 1 Corinthians 15:57

Colossians 2:13-15 • 1 John 5:4

Are there areas in your life where you currently feel defeated? **How can knowing that you are victorious in Him help you in your day to day life? Can you recall times that you were a victor because of Him?**

Daily Challenge:

#victorious

◯ Download "See a Victory" by Elevation Worship. Claim the words to this song as you remind yourself that victory is yours in Him. And remember to give Him the glory for every win you receive.

◯ Share a video, image, or your written testimony with other sisters in Christ in the "Because He Said So" Facebook group. Please use the hashtags #victorious and #iambecausehesaidso on all social media posts.

Visit Facebook.com/groups/iambecausehesaidso to join the community!

Day 31

I am...
FAVORED

"Surely, Lord, you bless the righteous; you surround them with your favor as with a shield."

Psalm 5:12

I was an elementary school teacher for 15 years and, although I loved every student that I ever taught and my intention was to treat every child the same, there were some students that were easier to build relationships with than others. These are the students whom we, as teachers, trust to deliver a note to the office or allow to help with other tasks and responsibilities in the classroom. These are the students who are often labeled as the "teacher's pet." The attributes that tend to cause a student to be placed in these types of leadership roles have to do with their attitude and actions. These students are generally the ones who bring smiles to their teachers' faces because they are rule-followers, they are responsible, and they treat others with kindness and respect, and I'm going to speak the truth here...it is hard not to show favoritism to these students who are so eager to please! When I was teaching, I prayed daily for God to show me ways to make every child feel special and loved.

In the Old Testament there is much to read about blessings and curses. It is quite clear that in order to receive God's blessings and favor, you had to keep the law perfectly! "If you fully obey the Lord your God and carefully follow all his commands, I give you today, the Lord your God will set you high above all the nations on earth. All these blessings will come on you and accompany you if you obey the Lord your God" (Deuteronomy 28:1-2). Praise be to the Lord! You can't lead a faultless life, but the sacrifice of Jesus blots out your sins; the blood of your Savior covers your imperfections. Because of the cross, God in His sovereignty, sees all of His children as His favorite. His favor, as the spotlight scripture points out, surrounds you like a shield. Isn't that a wonderful visual?

Favor is the undeserved goodness of God; it's the undeniable hand of your Creator orchestrating happenings in your life in ways that you can't comprehend.

Favor is the undeserved goodness of God; it's the undeniable hand of your Creator orchestrating happenings in your life in ways that you can't comprehend. Quite simply, favor is the grace and mercy poured out on you by God. It is favor that turns a shepherd to a king, it is favor that turns a prisoner to a prime minister, and it is favor that turns a young virgin girl into the mother of Jesus Christ. If you look closely at any of these "favored" characters from the Bible, you see that favor doesn't mean that you will never have battles to fight and storms to weather. It means that God will never leave your side during those difficult times.

How about you – do you want to be "THE Teacher's pet"; do you want God's favor on you? Do you desire to be the reason that He smiles? Do you want to please Him by seeking Him and taking steps of faith in obedience to that which He commands and calls you to do? "Those who seek the LORD lack no good thing" (Psalm 34:10). When you follow Jesus, favor follows you!

So today and every day moving forward, when your self-esteem is low, remember that you are surrounded like a shield with His favor. Claim that gift of favor shown to you as grace and mercy through Jesus and proclaim, **"I am favored...because He said so!"**

Prayer

Dear Lord, What a privilege it is to be favored by You. Thank You that You offer Your favor freely to all of Your children because You love us all equally. I am asking right now for Your favor on my life, my family, and my future so that I am always in the right place at the right time to be a blessing to others. In Jesus' name and for the Father's glory, Amen.

READ MORE
God's Word says you are favored...

Genesis 6:8   Psalm 30:5   Psalm 84:11

Psalm 90:17   Proverbs 3:4   Luke 1:28

Are you facing a stubborn or difficult circumstance that needs God's favor? **As a child of God, you can ask your "Abba" (Daddy) for anything. What outcome are you asking Him for?**

Daily Challenge:

#favored

☐ Buy or prepare a favorite treat or snack for someone special in your life. As you see the joy that this small gift brings to them, remember that this is how God delights in you.

☐ Share a video, image, or your written testimony with other sisters in Christ in the "Because He Said So" Facebook group. Please use the hashtags #favored and #iambecausehesaidso on all social media posts.

Visit Facebook.com/groups/iambecausehesaidso to join the community!

I am...
GIFTED

*"There are different gifts, but the same Spirit.
There are different ministries, but the same Lord.
There are different ways of working, but the same
God works all things in all men."*

1 Corinthians 12:4-5

It may have begun with "The Gong Show" and "Star Search,"
but "American Idol" was the spark that ignited a flame for a
smorgasbord of talent shows on television. Today, no station's
weekly line-up is complete without a show that judges gifted and
talented performers in hopes of discovering the next brilliant
superstar. If singing contests aren't your thing, you are sure to find
something that whets your appetite for a skill-based competition.
There are contest shows featuring dancers, chefs, bakers,
models, fashion designers, interior designers, athletes, builders,
landscapers, entrepreneurs, comedians, hair stylists, and even a
show that is searching to find an adult more intellectually skilled
than a 5th grader. I wonder if the reason we are so captivated by
these types of shows is because we love to watch gifted people

do their thing or if it makes us think about our own talents and how we are, or are not, using them.

Even as you are reading the words of this devotional, your mind may be wondering what talents you have and in what ways God has gifted you. I know this, Sister, you ARE talented. Everyone is! He has gifted you with your own unique set of skills based how He intends to use you for His kingdom. Perhaps your skills aren't in areas that can be put on a stage and applauded, but you can rest assured that you were given abilities and aptitudes that are divinely infused into your DNA for the purpose for which you were made. And you are called to use your gifts to glorify and honor Him!

To discover your gifts, you need to look deep inside your soul and ask what you are naturally good at—what you are happiest doing. You might not be good at singing, dancing, or acting, but you can perhaps plan, organize or decorate. You might not feel comfortable speaking, leading, or teaching, but you are right at home in a role where you encourage, listen or simply help others. You are uniquely created to play a role in the body of Christ.

If you compare your gifts and talents to the tools that one might use to build a house, it's easy to see how your individual giftedness is important in the collective construction of God's Kingdom. It is not a good idea to open a toolbox, grab the first tool that you find, and attempt to put a nail in the wall. Believe me, I

God gave you the gift of Jesus - the best gift of all. And He has gifted you with individual talents to be used for His glory. You were blessed with each gift to *be a gift.*

have tried it with a screwdriver, and it doesn't work! To effectively get a nail in a wall, you need the tool that was created for that purpose, a hammer. For you to be effective at accomplishing the purpose for which you have been created, you must claim the gifts you have been given and use them to the best of your ability to serve your Heavenly Father and others. "Each of you should use whatever gift you have received to serve others, as faithful stewards of God's grace in its various forms." (1 Peter 4:10).

God gave you the gift of Jesus—the best gift of all. And He also gifted you with individual talents to be used for His glory. You were blessed with each gift to BE a gift. Leo Buscaglia is quoted as saying, "Our talents are God's gifts to us, and what we do with them is our gift back to God."

So today and every day moving forward, when you give thanks to your Lord for the unique talents He has given you, praise Him for the plan that He has in your life. Find ways to use your giftedness for His glory and to bless others, as you gratefully acknowledge, "**I am gifted...because He said so!**"

Dear Lord, Forgive me when I don't recognize the abilities with which You have blessed me - both my natural talents and spiritual gifts. I give You all the glory for all the things that I can do well. Help me understand how to develop and use each gift for Your Kingdom. Lord, I also pray that You give me opportunities to use my gifts to be a gift to others. In Jesus' name and for The Father's glory, Amen.

READ MORE
God's Word says you are gifted...

Exodus 35:10 • Exodus 35:35

Romans 12:4-8 • Ephesians 2:10 • Ephesians 4:7

Do you struggle to recognize your own gifts and talents? **What have you identified as your natural talents and spiritual gifts? How are you using them to serve the Lord?**

_____

_____

_____

Daily Challenge:

#gifted

☐ God has blessed you with gifts so that you can share with others. Use your gifts today to bless someone around you. When they offer you praise for a job well done, give all the glory to God.

☐ Share a video, image, or your written testimony with other sisters in Christ in the "Because He Said So" Facebook group. Please use the hashtags #gifted and #iambecausehesaidso on all social media posts.

Visit Facebook.com/groups/iambecausehesaidso to join the community!

Day 33

I am...

CALLED

> *"And we know that in all things God works for the good of those who love him, who have been called according to his purpose."*
>
> **Romans 8:28**

Once upon a time, there were phones that were attached to a wall and served as the communication device for the entire family. These phones connected everyone to the outside world but required a hefty long-distance charge if you wanted to reach any place other than your local town or city. Worse yet, if you wanted to make a call, you had to wait your turn because your neighbors shared the same phone line. When this phone rang, and it rang loudly with no option to silence it, you couldn't just let it go to voicemail, because there was no such thing. If you didn't answer the call…you just missed it. Also, if you wanted to be the one to answer the call, you'd better be sitting closest to this phone and pick it up fast, or yell, "I've got it!" louder and more dramatically than anyone else in the house because there was always a race to say "hello". You actually had to answer this phone and wait to hear the voice on the other end of the line to know who was calling because Caller ID didn't exist. If you wanted any privacy when talking on this phone, you would stretch the coiled cord that connected the handset to the base as far as you could without pulling the machine off the wall. Then you had to shield the mouthpiece with your hand so no one else could hear what you were saying because you couldn't walk outside or to another room. This phone could not tell you the time or the weather forecast, however, you could dial a number to get a recording of the local time and temperature. This phone couldn't connect to the Internet, give you directions, or let you play games. It didn't even have a camera. This phone had one purpose—to send and receive calls.

You are called to give Him your heart and joyfully put Him before everything.

Wouldn't it be great if you heard the call on your life as loudly and clearly as the ring on an old family wall phone? You would hear the unmistakable voice of God coming through. You would listen and respond accordingly. But hearing God speak is not quite that easy. Samuel, a young boy who heard the audible voice of God, is a great example of this struggle. God had called out to him, called him by name three times. But it wasn't until the fourth time that Samuel recognized the voice of his Creator and replied, "Speak, your servant is listening" (Samuel 3:10b). It makes me wonder how often our God calls us to accomplish something for Him, but we don't recognize His voice, or we are too distracted by other voices around us.

Many people today are confused about their spiritual calling. They equate their calling with their career. I recently heard Steve Harvey say that your career is what you're paid for and your calling is what you're made for. I love that! And while it is true that numerous people's careers are in line with their calling, you are missing the mark if you feel your purpose is completely tied to your profession. It is not. In Matthew 22:36-37 Jesus is asked about the greatest commandment and replies that it is to love the Lord your God with all your heart and with all your soul and with all your mind. My sister in Christ, you are called to love God with a crazy love that inspires others to seek Him. You are called to give Him your heart and joyfully put Him before everything: "My son, give me your heart and let your eyes delight in my ways" (Proverbs 23:26).

You don't need to see God on your Caller ID to realize that He wants to communicate with you. When you are passionately pursing Him, you will find your purpose. His calling isn't always defined by huge life changes and decisions. Often it is found in the willingness to say "yes" to the less obvious choices you make to follow Him every day. Maybe you feel the Spirit prompting you to call a friend, treat the person behind you in the pick-up line to their lunch, or sit and listen caringly to a family member when you need to be completing a chore.

So today and every day moving forward, when He is calling you to something monumental like the mission field or something as seemingly mundane as to show compassion to someone in need, respond in obedience like Samuel. Knowing that you don't need a phone line for God to hear you, look up to Him and proclaim in His name, **"I am called...because He said so!"**

Prayer

> *Dear Lord, Forgive me for getting so busy that I don't hear You when You call. I want to be so sensitive to the promptings of the Holy Spirit that I immediately obey. I want others to be blessed through me. Show me my life's purpose as well as the small things You are calling me to do to help those around me. In Jesus' name and for the Father's glory, Amen.*

READ MORE

God's Word says you are called...

Genesis 6:22 • Genesis 12:4 • Philippians 3:14

1 Thessalonians 5:24 • 2 Timothy 1:9

Have you asked God to show you what He is calling you to do? **What are some of the things that you feel He has created you for and how can you take steps toward that calling now?**

Daily Challenge:

#called

☐ Call someone you love and trust. Ask them to pray with you about your calling. Even if you don't have clarity yet about the specifics of your calling, ask for His will to be done through you.

☐ Share a video, image, or your written testimony with other sisters in Christ in the "Because He Said So" Facebook group. Please use the hashtags #called and #iambecausehesaidso on all social media posts.

Visit Facebook.com/groups/iambecausehesaidso to join the community!

Day 34

I am...
EQUIPPED

*"His divine power has given us everything we
need for a godly life through our knowledge
of him who called us by his own glory and
goodness."*

2 Peter 1:3

Both my mother and my mother-in-law, Lottie Vance and Emily
Washam, are amazing cooks with huge hearts. I was so grateful
that they took turns to spend about a week with me after I
delivered each of my boys. While they came to spend special time
with the new babies, they were also willing to take on some of my
household roles while I adjusted to my "new normal". Although
they prepared some magnificent meals during their stay, I am sure
they felt somewhat handicapped in my kitchen because it was not
as fully equipped as what either were accustomed to. You see, I
am not much of a cook. Although I am a little more prepared now,
I definitely wasn't outfitted with the latest and greatest cooking
gadgets back then. I had only the bare necessities. I distinctly
remember my mom coming back from Walmart with the groceries

and baby supplies that were on the shopping list, as well as, a few new cooking tools. She couldn't help herself. She didn't want to get in the middle of cooking a meal and not be equipped to prepare it successfully.

In Christ you are equipped to do whatever you are called to do. Not because of *your* power, but because of *His*!

Yesterday's focus was your calling in Christ. Without a doubt, you want to be successful in that which He calls you to do. It has been said that God doesn't call the equipped, but He equips the called. Have you ever wondered why that is? I believe it is so that He gets all the glory. I believe that your calling will always be outside your comfort zone. It will always be too big for you to do alone by depending on your own natural talents and skills. It will cause you to depend fully on Him because you will not feel prepared to step into alone. That's where faith comes in. You must step forward in obedience and trust that God will provide for your every need to accomplish His purpose.

Moses, one of the most accomplished men in the Bible, was called by God to convince Pharaoh to set the Hebrew people free. However, he didn't feel equipped for the task. He wasn't confident in his ability to do that which he had been called to do. His gifts weren't in speaking and yet, that is exactly what God was calling him to do. As a matter of fact, Exodus 4:10 tells us that Moses was slow of speech and tongue. What God was asking him to do was very much out of his comfort zone. In Exodus 4:11-12 you read God's response. "The LORD said to him, 'Who gave human beings their mouths? Who makes them deaf or mute? Who gives them sight or makes them blind? Is it not I, the LORD? Now go; I will help you speak and will teach you what to say.'" God did exactly that.

When Jesus left earth and ascended to the heavenly realms, God graced you with the Holy Spirit, your Helper, to accomplish what you cannot do alone. "And if the Spirit of him who raised Jesus from the dead is living in you, he who raised Christ from the dead will also give life to your mortal bodies because of his Spirit who lives in you" (Romans 8:11). In Christ you are equipped to do whatever you are called to do. Not because of your power, but because of His!

My precious sister, rejoice! God equips you for your calling, and you can bet that you have everything you need to "cook up" something wonderful in His name. When you ask God to "show up and show out" in your life and to use you despite your weaknesses, He gets all the glory!

So today and every day moving forward, when you think about the things, big and small, that God is calling you to do, claim success in Jesus' name, and speak life into His plans saying confidently, "**I am equipped…because He said so!**"

Prayer

Dear Lord, Thank You for giving me all the tools that I could possible need to make a difference for Your Kingdom. Even when I feel inadequate and unprepared, I know that You have equipped me to do all that You are calling me to do. I give You all the glory because You make me able to do what I can't do on my own. In Jesus' name and for the Father's glory, Amen.

READ MORE

God's Word says you are equipped...

Exodus 4:1-11 • Luke 9:1-2 • Hebrews 13:20-21

1 Corinthians 1:26-29 • 2 Timothy 3:17

Do you feel you are fully equipped to serve Him and others? **What tools might you need to achieve His calling on your life? Who could you help knowing that you are equipped with all that you need?**

Daily Challenge:

#equipped

☐ During your morning routine, notice all of the tools that you use to help you look your best. Thank God for equipping you with all you need to do your best for Him.

☐ Share a video, image, or your written testimony with other sisters in Christ in the "Because He Said So" Facebook group. Please use the hashtags #equipped and #iambecausehesaidso on all social media posts.

Visit Facebook.com/groups/iambecausehesaidso to join the community!

Day 35

I am...
CONFIDENT

"But blessed is the one who trusts in the Lord, whose confidence is in him."

Jeremiah 17:7

I will never forget the Christmas that I got the beautiful pink bike with the white wicker basket attached to the handlebars. From the first moment I saw it, I could envision the great adventures it would take me on. I practiced for a few months on my training wheels, and in the spring, my daddy took them off. Finally, I was going to be able to ride off on my own! I imagined myself, hands high in the air, riding off into the sunset. I climbed up on the seat of that bike and, with my daddy's steady hand of support, I started pedaling. He was coaching me as we traveled up the gravel road. After a few minutes of his guidance I said, "I've got it. Let go!" And then…I fell; I fell hard! When I stood up the evidence of the fall was running down my leg, and I started crying. I wished that I could tell you that I got right back up on that bike and tried again. I wish I could tell you that I had great memories of experiences with my friends on our bike rides. But that would not be the truth. The truth is, I never learned to ride a bike. The truth is, I never had the confidence to get back on. The truth is, I missed out!

When I think of confidence displayed in the Bible, I think of a young boy with the slingshot and a pouch full of rocks who was confident that he could bring down the giant. In 1 Samuel 17:45, David, who had on no protective gear, looked up at the Philistine soldier named Goliath, who was dressed in full armor and said, "You come against me with sword and spear and javelin, but I come against you in the name of the Lord Almighty, the God of the armies of Israel, whom you have defied." These words made the oversized soldier angry, and he lunged after the boy. But the confident lad grabbed a rock from his bag and slung it into the forehead of his opponent, and down he went! David had defeated Goliath! WOW! If only you and I could have that kind of confidence when we are slaying the enemies we face today!

What would you be able to accomplish if you were truly confident, if you truly believed, that you can do all things through Him who strengthens you?

I'll say it again: You were created on purpose for a purpose. You may never step into that calling because you are afraid that you don't have all the answers. Unless you are confident that you can be successful, you might not even attempt that which you are called to do; you just won't. You are scared to step out of your comfort zone; you are afraid that you will fail. And if you do have the faith to try, but don't succeed on your first attempt, you may never "get back on that bike". When fear wins, you miss out! (Believe me, I know!). Isn't that just what the enemy wants? He wants you paralyzed by fear, He wants you to feel defeated. And he wants your belief that God has equipped you shut down so that you never accomplish what God is leading you to do.

You cannot depend on your own self-confidence to accomplish His commission on your life. But you can depend on Him. The confidence that you must have to live in the fullness of Christ and His calling for you can only be found at the cross.

It is said that learning to ride a bike is easy…once you stop worrying about falling off! Isn't that just as true when you consider living out the purpose of your life? Sister, you need to stop worrying about what might happen or that you might fail. You need to claim the promises found in Philippians 4:13. What would you be able to accomplish if you were truly confident, if you truly believed, that you can do all things through Him who strengthens you?

So today and every day moving forward, when insecurity is trying to invade your soul, stand tall. Don't be afraid of failing; move forward with all the confidence of Christ in you. Affirm that He didn't give you a spirit of timidity by positively proclaiming, "**I am confident…because He said so!**"

Prayer

Dear Lord, Forgive me when I try to live my life dependent on my own skills and abilities. I am so thankful that my competence and my confidence come from You. I realize that I can do nothing without You and everything through You. Lord, I pray specifically that You will give me the confidence to share Your love with those who need it. In Jesus' name and for the Father's glory, Amen.

READ MORE

God's Word says you are confident...

Psalm 27:3 • Proverbs 3:26 • 2 Corinthians 3:4

Ephesians 3:12 • Philippians 1:6

Hebrews 4:16 • 1 John 4:4

Have you ever failed at something and been hesitant to try again? **In what areas of your life do you lack confidence? In what areas do you feel confident? What can you accomplish for the Lord if you move forward in confidence in all areas, knowing that you can do all things through Christ?**

Daily Challenge:

#confident

☐ Write out Jeremiah 17:7 with your name in the blank, "But blessed is _____ who trusts in the LORD, whose confidence is in Him." Memorize this for when you or someone you know needs it.

☐ Share a video, image, or your written testimony with other sisters in Christ in the "Because He Said So" Facebook group. Please use the hashtags #confident and #iambecausehesaidso on all social media posts.

Visit Facebook.com/groups/iambecausehesaidso to join the community!

Day 36

I am a...
WARRIOR

"Yet, in all these things we are more than conquerors through him who loved us."

Romans 8:37

Oh, how I loved going to Vacation Bible School when I was growing up. I loved the stories, the snacks, and the arts and crafts. And, boy, did I love the songs! There were so many great ones that I still find myself humming now and again... "Jesus Loves Me," "Deep and Wide," "I've Been Redeemed," "Jesus Loves the Little Children," "He's Got the Whole World in His Hands," and "Down in my Heart," just to name a few. But there was one song, "Onward Christian Soldiers," that I never liked singing. I'm not sure if it was the song's slow tempo and heavy beat or the words about going to war; but I never really enjoyed that song.

My husband, Chris, is a history buff; he is especially interested in the wars and key battles from our country's past. Although I appreciate all those who have served in the armed forces and fought for my freedom, I have never enjoyed studying history, watching war documentaries, or spending vacation time going to war museums looking at artifacts from battles. I like peace, not war! So, to claim the role of Warrior for God, as He has commanded us to do, is really outside my comfort zone. But the truth is that we are in a battle with the enemy and we are called to fight! Peter didn't pull any punches when he described what we are up against: "Be alert and of sober mind. Your enemy the devil prowls around like a roaring lion looking for someone to devour. Resist him, standing firm in the faith, because you know that the family of believers throughout the world is undergoing the same kind of sufferings" (1 Peter 5:8-9). We need to realize that as women of Christ, wherever we are in the world, we are in constant combat with the evil one. Satan is determined to steal, kill, and destroy you by obliterating your confidence, shattering your hope, and exterminating your faith. His ultimate goal is to overthrow your relationship with God.

> My dear sister, you have been given a *divine order*, so don't leave your home without suiting up in the *full armor of God*.

As you have learned, you have a destiny, a calling in Christ, and the enemy will do anything in his power to stop you. You must be prepared to fight in the daily battle against the plans of evil. The only way to win the war with the enemy is to put on the full armor of God, every day! "Finally, be strong in the Lord and in His mighty power. Put on the full armor of God, so that you can take your stand against the devil's schemes. For our struggle is not against flesh and blood, but against the rulers, against the authorities, against the powers of this dark world and against the spiritual forces of evil in the heavenly realms. Therefore, put on the full armor of God, so that when the day of evil comes, you may be able to stand your ground, and after you have done everything, to stand. Stand firm then, with the belt of truth buckled around your waist, with the breastplate of righteousness in place, and with your feet fitted with the readiness that comes from the gospel of peace. In addition to all this, take up the shield of faith, with which you can extinguish all the flaming arrows of the evil one. Take the helmet of salvation and the sword of the Spirit, which is the word of God" (Ephesians 6:10-17).

My dear sister, you have been given a divine order, so don't leave your home without suiting up in the full armor of God. You don't want to enter the battlefield unprepared! Plan your own coup d'état against the devil! The good news is that you can fight confidently because the battle has been won; Jesus has already overcome! You have been called to share the good news of your Savior, not only by your words, but by your actions.

So today and every day moving forward, when worry wants to take over your world, sound the battle cry and tell the enemy, "Not today, devil, not today!" Then claim confidently, **"I am a warrior… because He said so!"**

Prayer

Dear Lord, Forgive me when I forget that Satan's goal is to steal, kill, and destroy. Make me spiritually sensitive and able to discern when I or someone I know is under the enemy's attack. Help me put on the whole armor of God so that I am ready to stand firm against the forces of evil. In Jesus' name and for the Father's glory, Amen.

READ MORE

God's Word says you are a warrior...

Judges 6:11-16 • Psalm 18:39 • Isaiah 42:13

2 Corinthians 10:3-4 • 1 Peter 5:7-9

Do you feel like a warrior or worrier on most days? **Reread Ephesians 6:10 - which pieces do you put on with ease and which pieces do you struggle with?**

Daily Challenge:

- ☐ At the end of this long day of worldly and spiritual battles...run a hot bath, pour in some bubbles, and turn up the praise music. Even the bravest warriors deserve some R&R.

- ☐ Share a video, image, or your written testimony with other sisters in Christ in the "Because He Said So" Facebook group. Please use the hashtags #warrior and #iambecausehesaidso on all social media posts.

Visit Facebook.com/groups/iambecausehesaidso to join the community!

Day 37

I am... INFLUENTIAL

"You are the salt of the earth. But if the salt loses its saltiness, how can it be made salty again? It is no longer good for anything, except to be thrown out and trampled underfoot."

Matthew 5:13

If you love chocolate the way I do, you are sure to want to cook up a batch of one of my family's old traditional recipes for your breakfast plate tomorrow: Cocoa and Biscuits. Some people call this dish, "Chocolate Gravy," but no matter the name of the recipe you use, if you love chocolate…you'd call it delicious. I have great memories of my mother cooking this wonderful treat for my family. Although I could sometimes talk her in to cooking it on a random weekend, it was primarily something that she prepared for special occasions, most specifically Christmas Eve. Early on in my marriage, I was excited to prepare this dish for my family and carry on the custom. (I believe that I have mentioned once or twice that I am not the best cook.) This recipe seemed easy enough so I thought I would give it a try. In addition to the cocoa, flour, sugar, milk, butter, and vanilla, it called for a pinch of salt. I wasn't exactly sure what a pinch of salt really looked like so the first time I prepared this delicacy, I added a very small sprinkling of salt. My results were not so good. It was definitely lacking in flavor. The next time I made it, I added too much salt; it was inedible. By the third time I made the dish, I had added the right amount of salt; and it was perfect. The amount of salt really influenced the dish—too little and it was bland; too much and it was a turnoff.

In today's spotlight scripture, you see that Jesus refers to His followers as the "salt of the earth." You may be wondering what this even means. Well, during the time when Jesus was delivering His famous Sermon on the Mount, salt was an extremely valuable commodity. It was not only used in seasoning food but also for preserving meat to keep it from rotting. Notice that Jesus says you ARE the salt. You don't have to become the salt; it is who you are in Him. As a follower of Christ, you are, like salt, extremely valuable. You are also called, through your influence, to serve as a seasoning agent and a preserving force in the world.

When you get out your saltshaker to let others see and taste life with Christ, remember to *be real*. When you authentically share all that God has done for you, *He* gets all the glory.

If you know Christ, you should live your life in a way that positively affects your family and friends, people in the workplace, and society as a whole. God wants to use you for His glory. You know all about the importance of having "good" influences in your life and of being a "good" influence on others. Sister, I don't know about you, but I am more interested in "God" influences! I want to be surrounded by Godly women who can season my walk with Him. I want to be that Godly example to those around me and do my part in preserving His kingdom.

When I was growing up, my grandmother always kept a salt substitute on the table. I am sure it had to do with cutting back on salt for health reasons, but I never liked the way it tasted. I always opened the cabinet and grabbed the real stuff. When you get out your saltshaker to let others see and taste life with Christ, remember to be real. When you authentically share all that God has done for you, He gets all the glory.

So today and every day moving forward, when you wonder what you have to offer, change your thinking and shake up your world a little bit. Sprinkle a little Jesus all around, and shout, "**I am influential…because He said so!**"

Prayer

Dear Lord, Remind me that wherever I go, I am influencing those around me. My words and actions either bring people closer to You or push them away. Help me "flavor" every situation, every conversation with Your grace. May I never miss the opportunity to "season" someone's life with the story of salvation through the Savior. In Jesus' name and for the Father's glory, Amen.

READ MORE

God's Word says you are influential...

Isaiah 42:6-7 • Mark 9:50

Mark 16:15 • Colossians 4:6

Do you consider yourself to be an influencer for God? **Can you think of times when you could have said something to "salt" the conversation and created a space to get your friends or family members thinking seriously about the Lord?**

Daily Challenge:

#influential

☐ Every time you salt your food today, think about how Christ expects us to flavor the world with His love. How can you sprinkle Jesus on those with whom you are sharing a meal?

☐ Share a video, image, or your written testimony with other sisters in Christ in the "Because He Said So" Facebook group. Please use the hashtags #influential and #iambecausehesaidso on all social media posts.

Visit Facebook.com/groups/iambecausehesaidso to join the community!

Day 38

I am...
RADIANT

"Those who look to him are radiant; their faces are never covered with shame."

Psalm 34:5

As I have mentioned before, when I was 3 years old, my mom divorced my biological father and left behind the abusive relationship that she had endured for 5 years. After the divorce it was just the two of us, and even though I had my own room and my own bed, I preferred to sleep with my mom. When she remarried the incredible man who became my daddy, it was time for me to be a big girl and start sleeping in my own bed. That is when I realized that I was scared of the dark. It didn't matter how calm I felt playing by myself in the same room before bed, once the lights went out, I was overcome with fear. Every shape in my closet became an evil monster and every creak in the house was a robber coming to get me. Finally, after many nights

153

of panic and tears, my mom wisely got me a nightlight. This little light, an invention from the 1960s, was a miracle. It calmed my imagination and helped me understand what was real and what was not. It gave me just enough light to make me feel secure in the darkness.

In Matthew 5:14-16 you read that you are called to be a light in the world's darkness: "You are the light of the world. A town built on a hill cannot be hidden. Neither do people light a lamp and put it under a bowl. Instead they put it on its stand, and it gives light to everyone in the house. In the same way, let your light shine before others, that they may see your good deeds and glorify your Father in heaven." Jesus declares in John 8:12 and 9:5 that He is the light of the world. And yet, if you look at the first seven words of the Matthew 5 passage above, Jesus is telling His followers, "You are the light of the world". That's you! Sister, when you follow Jesus, His light is in you and you are a light radiating in the world for Him.

> The Christian life is not about being private detectives for Jesus...You are not on a *secret* mission. You are meant to be a *beacon for all* to see Him in you.

Jesus continues his teaching by noting that "A town built on a hill cannot be hidden." The Greek word for "hidden" as it is written in this text is Krypta and it means "secret." Nobody builds a city on a hill expecting it to be a hidden fortress. If a city is built on a hill, you can see it from anywhere day or night. Similarly, when your life is built on Him, you can't keep it a secret....and you shouldn't. The Christian life is not about being private detectives for Jesus... You are not on a secret mission. You are meant to be a beacon for all to see Him in you.

Jesus concludes this section of scripture with an analogy that compares that city built on a hill to the light of a lamp. The purpose of a light is to illuminate, to help people see in the darkness.

Jesus' teaching of the city's purpose and the lamp's purpose should lead you to think about your purpose. Just like it would be crazy to light a lamp and cover it up, it's ludicrous to think that you should hide His light in you. Your purpose is to shine brightly and intentionally for Him.

You are called to go and illuminate the world so everyone can see the light, love, mercy, grace, and hope of Jesus. Christ is the source of all the light that radiates from you. When you plug into Him, you will glow with a light that will shine in someone's darkness illuminating their pathway to Christ.

So today and every day moving forward, when the world looks dim, sing out loud, "This little light of mine...I'm going to let it shine!". And beaming brightly in the light of Christ, keep singing in your spirit, **"I am radiant...because He said so!"**

Prayer

Dear Lord, Thank you for Your light, in me. Forgive me for the times that I've hidden my light because I wanted to fit in with the crowd or didn't want people to judge me. Help me, Father, to live my life so that it shines brightly with Your brilliance. I pray for ways to share Your light with everyone I meet so that they don't have to live in darkness. In Jesus' name and for the Father's glory, Amen.

READ MORE

God's Word says you are radiant...

Psalm 119:105 • Isaiah 60:1-2 • Matthew 5:16

John 8:12 • Acts 13:47 • Ephesians 5:8

Does the Light of Christ to radiate out from you? **What can you do to make sure that you are letting your light shine? Who do you know that needs His bright light shared with them today?**

Daily Challenge:

☐ Let God's light shine through you today. Do a random act of kindness today and tell the recipient that God loves them. Ask them to pass it on!

☐ Share a video, image, or your written testimony with other sisters in Christ in the "Because He Said So" Facebook group. Please use the hashtags #radiant and #iambecausehesaidso on all social media posts.

Visit Facebook.com/groups/iambecausehesaidso to join the community!

Day 39

I am...
COMPLETE

"For in Christ all the fullness of the Deity lives in bodily form, and in Christ you have been brought to fullness."

Colossians 2:9-10a

As a very young girl I can remember going to my aunt's house and watching her put together puzzles on the coffee table in her den. The puzzle box was always sitting nearby displaying what the current project would look like when it was all put together. The images were all beautiful and ranged from United States landmarks to exotic wildlife scenes. I remember being fascinated by how all of the pieces would fit together to make such a beautiful picture. My aunt would work on her puzzle for hours using skills like a detective to see which piece went where. The day she came home with a puzzle of Elvis, my cousins and I begged to help. My aunt seemed a little nervous with us kids wanting to participate, so she made her directions very clear: We were to sit still on the floor and only pick up one puzzle piece at a time. We understood; but after a while we found the restrictions too much and quickly fled for the trampoline. Wouldn't you know it, when the puzzle was nearly done, there was one piece missing. My aunt called us in to help her look for it. We searched and searched, but we could not find it. Finally, someone dug deep into the couch—and there it was! The piece that would complete the puzzle was found, placed where it belonged, and Elvis was complete.

Your life is much like that of a puzzle with missing pieces. You often waste time trying to find a way to put together all the pieces of your life so that your life looks as pretty as an image on a puzzle box. You are searching for the missing pieces to make you whole. You are looking high and low, and near and far, for the piece that will make your image complete. Life can be difficult. Sometimes it is really hard to see how all the pieces fit together. Sometimes it is challenging to find the missing piece. "The Lord is my portion; therefore, I will wait for him. The Lord is good to those whose hope is in him, to the one who seeks him" (Lamentations 3:24-25).

> You don't have to search! It is God who *completes you*. In the end, if you are *following* Him and *seeking* His will, your life will be an image of His beautiful work in you.

Sister, God is the missing piece! And unlike the story where my family was looking in the seemingly bottomless sofa for the piece to complete the Elvis puzzle, God is not hard to find. He is always there for you. You have a God-shaped hole in your soul that only He can fill, and that is a reason to rejoice! You don't have to search! It is He who completes you. In the end, if you are following Him and seeking His will, your life will be an image of His beautiful work in you. When you take the time to know Him deeper through His word and through prayer, you begin to see how all the pieces of your life fit together.

So today and every day moving forward, when you feel like you are inadequate, misplaced, incomplete and imperfect, make sure you have put in the missing piece to your life's puzzle. Let Jesus fill your soul! Then look in the mirror at the amazing masterpiece that He created you to be and declare, "**I am complete, because He said so!**"

Prayer

Dear Lord, Thank you for perfectly placing the pieces of my life together. I trust that even when I can't make sense of it all that You are creating something beautiful that will reflect You and Your love. I know for certain that I am complete in You, even if I can't see the final picture yet. Please use the pieces of my life to reveal Yourself to others. In Jesus' name and for the Father's glory, Amen.

READ MORE

God's Word says you are complete...

Psalm 138:8 • Psalm 139:16 • John 6:40

1 Corinthians 15:52 • 1 Thessalonians 5:23 • 1 John 2:5-6

Are you frustrated or discouraged with your life because you can't see the whole picture? **God will fill in the empty pieces. What parts of your life do you need to surrender to Him?**

Daily Challenge:

#complete

☐ What task, project, or goal in your life needs to be completed? Make a plan today to get it finished and ask God to help you. Give Him the glory when you are done.

☐ Share a video, image, or your written testimony with other sisters in Christ in the "Because He Said So" Facebook group. Please use the hashtags #complete and #iambecausehesaidso on all social media posts.

Visit Facebook.com/groups/iambecausehesaidso to join the community!

Day 40

I am...
UNFINISHED

"Being confident of this, that he who began a good work in you will carry it on to completion until the day of Christ Jesus."

Philippians 1:6

I love to go to the movies! There is not much I enjoy more than walking through the doors of the theatre, smelling the popcorn, finding the perfect seat (especially those new reclining ones), and waiting for the lights to go out and the trailers to begin. Admittedly, I fit in to that stereotypical female mold of moviegoers because my favorite films to watch are "chick flicks". You know, boy meets girl, boy and girl fall in love, boy and girl experience conflict, boy and girl make up and live happily ever after! Some of my all-time favorites are Dirty Dancing, Pretty Woman, Enchanted, The Wedding Planner, Sweet Home Alabama, Father of the Bride, and Pitch Perfect. What I love most about these types of movies is the happy ending! There is nothing as aggravating as investing two hours into watching a movie and being left with a cliffhanger never knowing what happens to the characters or how the story ends. It's as if the writer just left the script for the movie unfinished.

Yesterday, you learned that you are complete in Christ. But the fact that you woke up this morning means that He is not finished with you. God is still writing the script for your life. If you are breathing, He is busy directing you in the role in which you were cast, child of God. He has more in store for you; He is continually transforming you into what He wants you to become. Perhaps you've seen those buttons or bumper stickers that read: P.B.P.G.I.N.F.W.M.Y. This string of mysterious letters stands for an important truth: "Please be patient. God is not finished with me yet." Maybe you are still struggling when you look in the mirror to claim your starring role, your true identity in Christ, and that's okay! Show yourself some grace and remind yourself that He's still working on you! You are a work in progress!

My sweet sister, you've been on a 40-day journey to discover who you truly are in Christ. My prayer is that you have learned to see yourself the way God sees you, to forgive yourself the way God forgives you, to accept yourself the way God accepts you, and to love yourself the way God loves you. Knowing who you are in Him helps you understand the special role you play in this production called life! When you realize why you were created, you can rejoice in the uniqueness of your identity in God. When you have faith that your Creator is writing the perfect script for your life, you can get through any of life's struggles. Why? Because you are confident that you will have your "happily ever after" moment! No cliffhangers in your life! The sequel is certain — life with your Heavenly Father, forever!

> You've got more life to live *in* Him and *for* Him. Let's make *every* moment count!

In case you need a reminder, you are a masterpiece who is known, loved, rescued and chosen by the Creator of the Universe.

You are forgiven and found innocent, redeemed and transformed in His image; and you are free. You are healed, alive, approved, accepted, and invited by your Father to live life abundantly in Him. You are a princess who is wealthy, beautiful, cherished, and beloved. You are blessed, joyful, peaceful and enough. You are understood by your Maker, protected, fearless, courageous, strong, and victorious through the Savior. You are favored, gifted, called, and equipped so, therefore, you can be confident in every situation. You are a warrior who is influential and radiant. You are complete in Christ—however, He still is not done with you yet. Rejoice, my sister, the final credits haven't begun to roll! You've got more life to live in Him and for Him. Let's make every moment count!

So today and every day moving forward, when you feel like you've got nothing left to give, celebrate that God isn't finished with you yet. Knowing that He is the author of your story confidently declare, **"I am unfinished...because He said so!"**

Prayer

Dear Lord, You are The I AM and my identity, all that I am, is found only in You. Forgive me when I forget that You aren't finished with me yet. Until I am with You in Heaven, I am a work in progress. Help me to be more like You each day so that wherever I go or whatever I do, people will see You in my eyes. In Jesus' name and for the Father's glory, Amen.

READ MORE

God's Word says you are unfinished...

Psalm 23:6 ● Psalm 86:11-12 ● Luke 1:45

1 Corinthians 13:8-13 ● Philippians 3:12-14

1 Thessalonians 5:16-18 ● Hebrews 3:15

Are you excited that God has more plans for you? **What are you hoping for? What does the next season of your life look like? What do you need to believe and take action on...***because He said so*?

Daily Challenge:

#unfinished

☐ Download the song "Unfinished" by Mandisa and let the lyrics fill your soul. Listen to it today and as often as possible moving forward to remind yourself that God isn't finished with you yet.

☐ Share a video, image, or your written testimony with other sisters in Christ in the "Because He Said So" Facebook group. Please use the hashtags #unfinished and #iambecausehesaidso on all social media posts.

Visit Facebook.com/groups/iambecausehesaidso to join the community!

Daily
"GOD-FIRMATIONS"

I am...
KNOWN

I am...
CHOSEN

I am a...
MASTERPIECE

I am...
LOVED

"O LORD, you have examined my heart and know everything about me."

Psalm 139:1

"Therefore, as God's chosen people, holy and dearly loved, clothe yourselves with compassion, kindness, humility, gentleness and patience."

Colossians 3:12

"For we are God's masterpiece. He has created us anew in Christ Jesus, so we can do the good things he planned for us long ago."

Ephesians 2:10

"For God so loved the world that he gave his one and only Son, that whoever believes in him shall not perish but have eternal life."

John 3:16

I am...
RESCUED

I am...
FORGIVEN

I am...
INNOCENT

I am...
REDEEMED

"In Him we have redemption through His blood, the forgiveness of our trespasses, according to the riches of His grace."

Ephesians 1:7

"I have swept away your offenses like a cloud, your sins like the morning mist. Return to me, for I have redeemed you."

Isaiah 44:22

"I waited patiently for the Lord; he turned to me and heard my cry. He lifted me out of the slimy pit, out of the mud and mire; he set my feet on a rock and gave me a firm place to stand."

Psalm 40:1-2

"Their sins and their lawless deeds I will remember no more."

Hebrews 10:17

I am...
FREE

I am...
ALIVE

I am...
TRANSFORMED

I am...
HEALED

"If the Son sets you free, you will be free indeed."

John 8:36

"But because of His great love for us, God, who is rich in mercy, made us alive with Christ, even when we were dead in our trespasses. It is by grace you have been saved."

Ephesians 2:4-5

"Do not conform to the pattern of this world but be transformed by the renewing of your mind. Then you will be able to test and approve what God's will is, his good, pleasing and perfect will."

Romans 12:2

"Heal me, Lord, and I will be healed; save me and I will be saved, for you are the one I praise."

Jeremiah 17:14

I am...
APPROVED

I am...
ACCEPTED

I am...
INVITED

I am a...
PRINCESS

"To the praise of the glory of his grace, wherein he hath made us accepted in the beloved."

Ephesians 1:6 (KJV)

"So, in Christ Jesus you are all children of God through faith."

Galatians 3:26

"But just as we have been approved by God to be entrusted with the gospel, so we speak, not as pleasing men, but God who examines our hearts."

1 Thessalonians 2:4

"Come to me, all you who are weary and burdened, and I will give you rest."

Matthew 11:28

I am...
WEALTHY

I am...
BEAUTIFUL

I am...
CHERISHED

I am...
BELOVED

*You are altogether beautiful;
there is no flaw in you."*

Song of Solomon 4:7

---

*"So, you are no longer a slave,
but God's child; and since you
are his child, God has made you
also an heir."*

Galatians 4:7

---

*"For I am convinced that neither
death, nor life, nor angels, nor
principalities, nor things present,
nor things to come, nor powers,
nor height, nor depth, nor any other
created thing, will be able to separate
us from the love of God, which is in
Christ Jesus our Lord."*

Romans 8:38-39

---

*"She is worth far more than
rubies."*

Proverbs 31:10

I am...
JOYFUL

I am...
ENOUGH

I am...
BLESSED

I am...
PEACEFUL

"When anxiety was great within me, your consolation brought joy to my soul!"

Psalm 94:19

"Whom have I in heaven but you? And earth has nothing I desire besides you. My flesh and my heart may fail, but God is the strength of my heart and my portion forever."

Psalm 73:25-26

"Blessed is she who believed that He would fulfill His promises to her."

Luke 1:45

"You will keep in perfect peace those whose minds are steadfast, because they trust in you."

Isaiah 26:3

_I am..._
UNDERSTOOD

_I am..._
PROTECTED

_I am..._
FEARLESS

_I am..._
COURAGEOUS

"The LORD will keep you from all harm-- he will watch over your life;"

Psalm 121:7

"You know when I sit down and when I rise up; you discern my thoughts from afar."

Psalm 139:2

"Be strong and courageous. Do not be afraid or terrified because of them, for the LORD your God goes with you; he will never leave you nor forsake you."

Deuteronomy 31:6

"For God has not given us a spirit of fear, but of power and of love and of a sound mind."

2 Timothy 1:7

I am...
STRONG

I am...
VICTORIOUS

I am...
FAVORED

I am...
GIFTED

"But thanks be to God! He gives us the victory through our Lord Jesus Christ."

1 Corinthians 15:57

"But you, Lord, do not be far from me. You are my strength; come quickly to help me."

Psalm 22:19

"There are different gifts, but the same Spirit. There are different ministries, but the same Lord. There are different ways of working, but the same God works all things in all men."

1 Corinthians 12:4-5

"Surely, Lord, you bless the righteous; you surround them with your favor as with a shield."

Psalm 5:12

_I am..._
EQUIPPED

_I am a..._
WARRIOR

_I am..._
CALLED

_I am..._
CONFIDENT

"His divine power has given us everything we need for a godly life through our knowledge of him who called us by his own glory and goodness."

2 Peter 1:3

"Yet, in all these things we are more than conquerors through him who loved us."

Romans 8:37

"And we know that in all things God works for the good of those who love him, who have been called according to his purpose."

Romans 8:28

"But blessed is the one who trusts in the Lord, whose confidence is in him."

Jeremiah 17:7

I am...
INFLUENTIAL

I am...
RADIANT

I am...
COMPLETE

I am...
UNFINISHED

"Those who look to him are
radiant; their faces are never
covered with shame."

Psalm 34:5

"Being confident of this, that
he who began a good work in
you will carry it on to completion
until the day of Christ Jesus."

Philippians 1:6

"You are the salt of the earth.
But if the salt loses its saltiness,
how can it be made salty
again? It is no longer good for
anything, except to be thrown
out and trampled underfoot."

Matthew 5:13

For in Christ all the fullness of
the Deity lives in bodily form,
and in Christ you have been
brought to fullness."

Colossians 2:9-10a

Appendix 1

"My Mama"
By: Missy
Christmas 1972

Appendix 2

SNACK 'N SMILE BAGS
Instructions

"For I was hungry and you gave me food, I was thirsty and you gave me drink, I was a stranger and you welcomed me."

Matthew 25:35

Snack 'n Smile bags are a "God idea" birthed in 2017, in Sarasota, by my dear friend and Soul Sister, Anne Ayres. God has richly blessed Anne with creative ideas that have eternal impact. She is very intentional about taking action to that which He has called her to do.

Snack 'n Smile bags are created to be handed out to those in need. These bags are simply that…a snack and a smile! In each brown bag is a water bottle, cheese/peanut butter crackers, applesauce, granola/protein bar, napkin, spoon, sanitizer wipe, gum/mint and an inspirational message (purchased or handwritten). One side of the bag says "Snack 'n Smile" with a smiley face and the other side says "God loves you!" with a heart.

These bags can be made ahead and kept in a basket in your car so that you are ready when prompted to give! They can also be made "assembly style" with your family or with a small group and can be given to an organization that serves the homeless community in your hometown. Snack 'n Smiles are simply a way to be a vessel of God's love to those that perhaps are hungry, thirsty or in need of a smile.

Appendix 3

Sister, if you've never asked Jesus into your heart, it is as easy as repeating the words of this prayer. If you already walk with Jesus, you can use this as a prayer of praise as you remember the incredible gift Jesus gave you through His sacrifice.

The Salvation Prayer

Dear Lord Jesus,

*Come into my life today. I believe in
You and receive Your gift of grace.
Forgive me of my sins and make me
a new person from the inside out.*

*In Jesus' name I pray,
Amen.*

If you just repeated these words, let me be the first to welcome you to the family of God. Sister, buckle your seatbelt, because your life will never be the same.

Appendix 4

The Lord's Prayer

Our Father in Heaven,
hallowed be your name,
your kingdom come,
your will be done,
on earth as it is in Heaven.
Give us this day our daily bread.
And forgive us of our debts,
as we have forgiven our debtors.
And lead us not into temptation,
but deliver us from evil.
For yours is the kingdom,
and the power, and the glory forever.
Amen.

Appendix 5

The Prayer of
St. Assisi

Lord, make me an instrument of your peace:
where there is hatred, let me sow love;
where there is injury, pardon;
where there is doubt, faith;
where there is despair, hope;
where there is darkness, light;
where there is sadness, joy.

O Divine Master, grant that I may
not so much seek
to be consoled as to console,
to be understood as to understand,
to be loved as to love.
For it is in giving that we receive,
it is in pardoning that we are pardoned,
and it is in dying that we are born to eternal life.
Amen.

Appendix 6

Chocolate Pudding Family Recipe

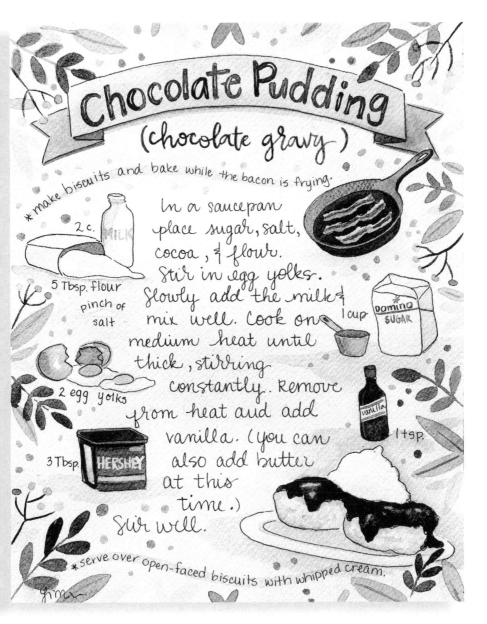

Chocolate Pudding (chocolate gravy)

* make biscuits and bake while the bacon is frying.

2 c. MILK
5 Tbsp. flour
pinch of salt
2 egg yolks
3 Tbsp. HERSHEY
1 cup Domino SUGAR
vanilla 1 tsp.

In a saucepan place sugar, salt, cocoa, & flour. Stir in egg yolks. Slowly add the milk & mix well. Cook on medium heat until thick, stirring constantly. Remove from heat and add vanilla. (You can also add butter at this time.) Stir well.

* serve over open-faced biscuits with whipped cream.

Art by Laura Moore

Discovering Who the _I AM Says I Am_

📱 GET SOCIAL!

FACEBOOK
Connect with sisters in Christ in the "Because He Said So" Facebook group. To join the group, visit Facebook.com/groups/iambecausehesaidso

INSTAGRAM
Follow @IAmBecauseHeSaidSo on Instagram for continual encouragement.

WEBSITE
Visit www.IAmBecauseHeSaidSo.com for more resources.

Connect with Missy!

Missy Washam was born with a passion for people and a giftedness to encourage, inspire, and motivate others to be their best self. This educator turned entrepreneur is now certified and licensed as a speaker, trainer, and coach and helps people connect the dots between their passion and purpose. Missy serves on the International Support Committee for the International Foundation for Women's Empowerment. Missy is Co-founder and Executive Director for Soul Sisters Ministry which encourages women of faith from all over the world. Missy resides in Clinton, Mississippi with her husband, Chris, where they attend First Baptist Church. Missy loves Jesus and has a passion for helping people *believe* that they are created **on** purpose and **for** a purpose.

Invite Missy to your next event or conference. She speaks on a variety of topics and can tailor a message for your group's need. Reach out today to learn more.

Missy 🅜 *Washam*

Facebook:	Facebook.com/MissyMotivates
Website:	www.MissyWasham.com
Email:	missy@missywasham.com
Phone:	(601) 927-6464

Made in the USA
Monee, IL
26 March 2021